MW00527956

THE
SINKING
OF THE
STEAMBOAT
LEXINGTON
ON
LONG ISLAND SOUND

BILL BLEYER

THE
History
PRESS

Published by The History Press
Charleston, SC
www.historypress.com

Copyright © 2023 by Bill Bleyer
All rights reserved

First published 2023

Manufactured in the United States

ISBN 9781467150286

Library of Congress Control Number: 2022950430

Notice: The information in this book is true and complete to the best of our knowledge. It is offered without guarantee on the part of the author or The History Press. The author and The History Press disclaim all liability in connection with the use of this book.

All rights reserved. No part of this book may be reproduced or transmitted in any form whatsoever without prior written permission from the publisher except in the case of brief quotations embodied in critical articles and reviews.

CONTENTS

ACKNOWLEDGEMENTS

Stephen Goldman; Tod Thonger; Robert Wass; Ben Roberts of Eastern Search & Survey; John Beninati; James Brust; Brian E. O'Connor; Kim Barteau, Karen Liotta, Selina Ferragamo and Barbara Compono of the Bayville Free Library; Captain Steve Bielenda; Killian Taylor of the Suffolk County Vanderbilt Museum & Planetarium; Lauren Brincat of Preservation Long Island; Adam Grohman of the Underwater Historical Research Society; Jaime Karbowiak of the Long Island Maritime Museum; Karen Martin of the Huntington Historical Society; Elizabeth A.S. Beaudin at the Pequot Library in Southport, Connecticut; Reed Sparling of Scenic Hudson; Mark Munro and John Stanford of Sound Underwater Survey; Tim Coleman; Green-Wood Cemetery historian Jeffrey I. Richman; Cassie Ward of the Putnam History Museum; David Oat of the Norwich Historical Society; Jennifer Galpern and J.D. Kay of the Rhode Island Historical Society; Ilena Andrews of PBA Galleries; losttosight.com; Heather Johnson; Annalisa Heppner and Marcello Penta of the North Burial Ground in Providence, Rhode Island; the Fall River (Massachusetts) Historical Society; Linda Liguori of the Harrison (New Jersey) Public Library; Deanna Witte-Walker and Amy Folk of the Southold Historical Society; Stephen Sullivan and Kay Simpson of Springfield Museums; Astrid Drew of the Steamship Historical Society; Maribeth Quinlan and Claudia Triggs of Mystic Seaport Museum; L. Sanford Rice III of the Society of the Cincinnati in the State of New Jersey; and Harry Newman of the Old Print Shop.

My reviewer/proofreaders: Joe Catalano and Natalie Naylor for reading the entire manuscript and Tod Thonger, James Brust, Robert Wass, Robert MacKay and Adam Grohman for some chapters.

And my editors at The History Press: Banks Smither and Abigail Fleming.

INTRODUCTION

Other than a small group of Long Island and Connecticut historians, maritime researchers and scuba divers as well as some lithograph collectors, few people today have heard of the fire that consumed and sank the steamboat *Lexington* on Long Island Sound in 1840. But at the time, the disaster—which still holds the record for the worst loss of life on the waters surrounding what most people consider to be Long Island (Nassau and Suffolk Counties)—was major news that captivated the public.

This notoriety was the result, to a large degree, of a lithograph of the blazing vessel produced by the firm of young entrepreneur Nathaniel Currier, which was one of the first images to run in a daily newspaper extra edition when published by the New York *Sun* and then by Currier.

Memory of the *Lexington* would be overshadowed by maritime disasters with far greater death tolls, including the fire that destroyed the steamboat *General Slocum* on the East River in 1904, the sinking of the White Star liner *Titanic* in 1912 and the torpedoing of the *Lusitania* in 1915. But the horrible deaths by flames or frigid water of all but 4 of the up to 150 passengers and crew aboard the *Lexington* on the night of January 13–14, 1840, filled newspapers and captivated their readers for weeks. The amazing stories of the 4 survivors also generated huge public interest. Not surprisingly, the public and an inquest jury wanted to place blame and designate heroes and villains—and they did.

But even with the uproar over the sinking and the perceived lack of adequate safety equipment and training for the crew, it would take another dozen years and more similar disasters before safety regulations were strengthened by Congress.

Despite growing up on the shore of Long Island Sound and being a maritime history buff since childhood, I had not heard of the *Lexington* until researching shipwrecks as a *Newsday* staff writer working in the late 1990s on the "Long Island: Our Story" project, which spun out the history of the region in daily stories over the course of a year with portions later reprinted in three books.

There have been many tragic shipwrecks around Long Island dating back to at least the 1657 loss off Fire Island of the *Prins Maurits* carrying colonists to what would become Delaware, but none produced as high a loss of life and dramatic survival stories as the ill-fated steamboat.[1] I cover shipwrecks around Long Island in my earlier book *Long Island and the Sea: A Maritime History* (The History Press, 2019) and leave New York City shipwrecks, such as the 1904 fire and sinking of the excursion steamer *General Slocum* in the East River with the deaths of 1,021 passengers and crew, to other authors.

I have written about the floating palace built by Cornelius Vanderbilt in 1835 in recent years in *Newsday* and *Long Island and the Sea*, but I'm delighted to have finally accumulated enough information to turn the story into its own book. I hope readers will find it worth the effort.

1

EARLY STEAMBOATS
ON LONG ISLAND SOUND

The earliest travel between Long Island and Connecticut or Long Island and Manhattan and beyond was done by Native Americans using dugout canoes. Later in the colonial period, marine transportation relied on sail power. In the eighteenth century, moving people and goods by water became more predictable with the introduction of ferries powered by horses walking on treadmills to turn paddlewheels. But while faster and more reliable, horse-propelled ferries were not immune to mishaps. In 1741, one of these ferries that had been running successfully from what is today Lattingtown on Long Island to Rye in Westchester County, New York, capsized in a storm. Thomas Jones of Oyster Bay had operated the ferry for two years when he, his Black helper, five passengers and six horses drowned.[2]

A ticket for the ferry *Nassau*, which traveled between Brooklyn and Manhattan in 1814. *From* Harper's Weekly, *1872.*

Maritime travel became even more reliable with the introduction of steam power, although boilers added the risk of fire and explosions, which occurred frequently. Robert Fulton and his financial backer, Robert Livingston, initiated steam-powered ferry service between Manhattan and Brooklyn in 1814. When their *Nassau* made its maiden voyage on May 10, the *Long Island Star* reported enthusiastically that "this noble boat surpassed the expectations of the public in the rapidity of her movements." Trips across the East River lasted between five and twelve minutes, depending on tide and weather. On the inaugural day, the *Nassau* carried 549 passengers, some of whom purchased ten-dollar annual commutation tickets.[3]

THE STEAMBOAT CONNECTION TO NEW ENGLAND

Only a year after the debut of the *Nassau*, there was another major development in marine transportation for the region. On March 21, 1815, Captain Elihu S. Bunker navigated the first steam-powered vessel through the treacherous rocks and whirlpools of Hell Gate on the East River between Queens and Randall's Island and into Long Island Sound. The 134-foot *Fulton* was owned by and named for Robert Fulton, who had launched the vessel the previous year to operate on the Hudson River. It was eight years after Fulton operated the first successful steamboat on the Hudson. With its top speed of eight miles per hour, the steamboat required eleven hours to complete the seventy-five-mile trip to New Haven, Connecticut. The *Fulton* was powered by a large, noisy engine centered between two paddlewheels. Although passengers were crowded into a small cabin toward the stern, business boomed. Despite their slow pace, Bunker's early voyages were a breakthrough that led to the next milestone in transportation on Long Island Sound: regularly scheduled steamboat service.

Later in 1815, Bunker began piloting the *Fulton*, which was rigged as a sloop in case sails were needed—as they often were—up the Connecticut River to Hartford. The *Hartford Courant* wrote enthusiastically that "it is hardly possible to conceive that anything of its Kind can exceed her, in elegance and convenience." After service was extended to New London, President James Monroe took advantage of the *Fulton* when he toured New England in March 1817.[4] When the *Fulton* extended service from New York to Providence in 1821, the eighty passengers on the inaugural run included Secretary of State John Quincy Adams.[5]

In the early days of Long Island Sound steamboat service, the passengers were more interested in traveling between New York and Boston than to destinations in between. Before the Cape Cod Canal opened in 1914, passengers avoided going all the way between New York and Boston by water because it required a frequently rough ocean voyage around Cape Cod. That was the route followed by "packet," or regularly scheduled, ships before the advent of steam power. To avoid Cape Cod, the early steamboat lines began running from Manhattan to New England coastal cities from New Haven, Connecticut, to New Bedford, Massachusetts, where they could connect with stagecoaches and later train lines. The alternative was making the trip the only way possible before the arrival of the steamboats: a four-day stagecoach ride with three short overnight sleeping stops.[6]

New York State awarded Fulton's company exclusive rights to operate steamboats in its waters. Connecticut retaliated by refusing to permit Fulton's line to operate within its waters. That forced the New York company to run on the Long Island side of the Sound, out to Narragansett Bay in Rhode Island and up to Providence. That turned out to be the fastest route to Boston. But it still meant an overnight trip of about twelve hours on the water plus six hours riding in a stagecoach from Providence to Boston, not counting stops for dinner or changing horses.[7]

The boilers on the early steamboats consumed cords of wood so quickly that the captains would pick up schooners full of extra fuel off Fishers Island and tow them to refuel without stopping. That cumbersome procedure was eliminated with a successful trial of a coal-fired boiler in 1836. Unfortunately, the existing boilers were not designed to contain the sustained higher pressure from coal fires, resulting in an increased rate of explosions and deaths. The problem was exacerbated by captains racing to gain bragging rights and, hopefully, more passengers because of shorter travel times. In one widely publicized accident, the sidewheeler *New England* exploded on the Connecticut River after successfully racing the *Providence* down the Sound in 1833. When two boilers exploded, fifteen people died immediately or later from their injuries. Some captains attempted to reduce the anxiety over boiler explosions by placing their passengers on a sailing vessel and then towing it behind the steamboat. Other companies attempted a design remedy by relocating the boiler from the hold to the upper deck so that if it exploded, the force would go upward.[8]

In 1824, the Supreme Court ruled that state-granted monopolies were unconstitutional. The decision led to a golden age of steamboat travel on what became known as the "American Mediterranean." By the end of the decade, competition had become cutthroat, with companies offering lower fares, luxury accommodations and higher speeds than other lines. The higher speeds, naturally, resulted in more boiler explosions until engineers devised new boilers that could withstand the higher pressure generated by coal fires.[9]

2

"COMMODORE"
CORNELIUS VANDERBILT

Following the Supreme Court's 1824 anti-monopoly ruling, many entrepreneurs entered the newly competitive steamboat business. The one who would become the most famous was Cornelius Vanderbilt. Dubbed "The Commodore" by a newspaper, Vanderbilt started out as a boatman in New York Harbor before beginning a three-decade career operating steamboats, initially on the Hudson River, then the rougher waters—both in terms of nature and competition—of Long Island Sound.

The son of Cornelius Vand Derbilt, later changed to Vanderbilt, and Phebe Hand was born on Staten Island on May 27, 1794. He was one of nine children of a poor farm family in Port Richmond. With little income gleaned from the rocky soil, the elder Cornelius took whatever odd jobs he could find around the waterfront.[10]

The Vanderbilt children literally grew up on the waterfront....Cornelius... took to water like a duck....He excelled in the accomplishments of a robust boy. He would swim farthest in the surf and row farthest out to sea.... He had a quick eye for sailing vessels; as a child he could distinguish the difference between a bark and a ship, a schooner and a brigantine. Soon he knew by sight every large vessel belonging to the port, and learned the rig and outline of every fishing-smack...that entered the harbor. Like most of the farmers along the shore, old Cornelius...owned a small sailboat to carry produce to the city market. Soon young Cornele [as he was known], *even before he reached his teens, was entrusted with the boat.*[11]

Cornelius Vanderbilt photographed in middle age by the famous studio of Mathew Brady. *Library of Congress.*

"He sailed like a master at an early age," biographer Edward J. Renehan Jr. wrote. "Always large and well-muscled for his years, he was a strong rower, and he won many a local race."[12]

In 1810, when he was sixteen, Cornelius told his mother that he wanted to go to sea, something she discouraged because of the dangers and hardships. Instead, they agreed that he could have his own boat. In the Port Richmond neighborhood, a small two-masted flat-bottomed vessel called a periauger was for sale for $100. It was agreed that Cornelius could plant corn on a family plot that had never been farmed because it was so stony and use the proceeds of the crop to pay off a loan from his parents to buy the boat, according to family folklore, or just be paid $100 outright for undertaking the project, as Vanderbilt told the story later in life. Like Tom Sawyer, he persuaded his friends to help with the project by telling them that they would be allowed to sail with him.[13]

Years later, Vanderbilt reminisced, "I didn't feel as much satisfaction when I made two million…as I did on that bright May morning sixty years before when I stepped onto my own periauger, hoisted my own sail, and put my hand on my own tiller."[14]

Once the boat was ready, early biographer Wheaton Lane wrote, "Young Vanderbilt, known as 'Cornele, the Boatman,' ferried passengers between Stapleton on Staten Island and Whitehall Landing near the southern tip of Manhattan in the morning and carried them back at the end of the day. Some were regular commuters, others farmers going to the city to purchase supplies. Like his father before him, he had competition, although his father had quit the business because he found the competition too stiff." The younger Vanderbilt succeeded because he provided reliable service on a strict schedule and he always sailed, whatever the weather. He was considered the best sailor in the harbor and made the seven-mile trip faster than anyone else. If the wind died when he was in shallow water, he would use a pole to push his craft to the dock. He would often carry freight as long as he could keep his passenger schedule. His passengers found his manner curt or even rude, but he seemed not to care and succeeded by his ambition and undercutting his competitors on fares, biographers agree.[15]

"The young man was selling transport, not conversation," Renehan wrote. "He was also passionate about commanding his craft efficiently and maximizing its profitability, often at the expense of politeness and passenger comfort. Gruff, severe, and sure of himself as a youth, Vanderbilt was to remain so all his life: never suffering fools gladly, always going his own way, and always looking out for himself first."[16]

While Lane and some other early historians claimed Vanderbilt and even his father ran ferry service from Staten Island to Manhattan on a regular schedule, Renehan said there was no proof of that and that he probably carried cargo and passengers as he found them.[17]

Vanderbilt's hard work paid off. He sailed whenever he had customers, regardless of the weather, and always undercut the prices of competitors—a trend that would continue for his entire business career. By the end of his first season, he had a $1,000 profit. He shared his proceeds with his parents but was still able to buy an interest in two other periaugers—the beginning of his career as an investment capitalist.[18]

The War of 1812 brought Vanderbilt more business ferrying soldiers and provisions to forts around the harbor, although it meant he was working around the clock. After the war, he bought a sixty-five-foot government-surplus schooner for $1,500 in cash for carrying cargo along the coast. He recouped the money in one trip by bringing oysters through a fierce storm from Chesapeake Bay to New York faster than any of his competitors. Vanderbilt then focused entirely on the coastal trade and left the harbor ferrying to a subordinate. He continued to acquire sloops and periaugers, sometimes with investments from his father. When he had a vessel built for him, he provided the specifications, showing a natural flair for boat design. The first boat built for him—in 1813, when he was nineteen—was the *Swiftsure*, constructed at a New Jersey shipyard. Within seven years, he had acquired $15,000 in cash and assets. At that point, his interest shifted from sail to steam vessels.[19]

Steam power around New York Harbor was not a new phenomenon when Vanderbilt began gravitating in that direction in 1817. It was a decade after Robert Fulton famously had successfully operated the *Clermont* on the Hudson River, following John Fitch's earlier operation of a steamboat on the Delaware River that had successfully covered about two thousand miles of scheduled trips.[20]

In 1787, Fitch launched a paddlewheel steamer, a sixty-foot vessel that could carry thirty passengers. It was later used commercially on a run between Philadelphia and Burlington, New Jersey. Eventually, the New York State legislature granted Fitch an exclusive license to run steamboats on New York waters. That license was repealed in March 1798 when the legislature transferred the rights to one of its own members, Robert Livingston, who had been funding Fulton's work.

James Rumsey, another American inventor, built a steamboat even simpler than Fitch's that he launched on the Potomac River in 1787, but it was never

Aaron Ogden, a New Jersey governor and steamboat entrepreneur. *Library of Congress.*

used commercially. In 1804, John Stevens of New Jersey built a small steamboat with twin screw propellers named *Little Juliana* after his daughter and ran it on the Hudson with modest success. Five years after that, Stevens launched the *Phoenix*, a paddlewheel steamboat he used on a voyage from New York City to Philadelphia, which was the first ocean trip ever made by a steamboat, and then used it as a ferry between Manhattan and Hoboken, New Jersey.[21]

Initially, Vanderbilt showed little interest in steamboats, sharing the belief of other sailing men that the new contraptions were unreliable and too expensive to operate profitably. But his thinking changed as the steamboats were built with more powerful engines and began to run more reliably on the Hudson River and Long Island Sound. They eclipsed sailing vessels on their routes, especially when the *Nautilus* began making trips in 1817 between Staten Island and New York. Eventually, Vanderbilt booked a round trip up the Hudson to Albany on one of Livingston's steamboats to study the equipment. He concluded that steam represented the future of maritime transportation.[22]

With Livingston's monopoly on steam navigation in New York, other operators were forced to pay him a royalty to navigate those waters. The competitors challenged the monopoly repeatedly. One was Aaron Ogden of New Jersey, a lawyer who was elected governor in 1812. The New Jersey legislature granted Ogden exclusive use of steamboats in that state's waterways, creating an impasse for vessels operating in New York Harbor between the two states. Ogden, in turn, was challenged by Thomas Gibbons, a wealthy lawyer and planter who had moved from Savannah to New Jersey a few years earlier. He started out as a business partner with Ogden on a sail ferry between New Jersey and New York, but the two soon had a falling out. Gibbons then challenged his former partner's monopoly, ultimately resulting in the Supreme Court ruling in *Gibbons v. Ogden* that interstate commerce was controlled by the federal government and not the states. Gibbons became Vanderbilt's first and only employer.[23]

Even though Gibbons could not acquire a license to operate, he was determined to take on Ogden and acquired a small sidewheeler steamboat named *Stoudinger*. To run the boat, he wanted a captain who would not be intimidated by the monopolies in either state and so hired Vanderbilt in 1818.[24]

Vanderbilt sold his sloop and schooners, yielding about $7,000. He kept one of the old periaugers, which he, his father or brother Jacob would run occasionally between Staten Island and Manhattan.[25]

Vanderbilt had been earning $3,000 a year on his coastal trips but agreed to work for Gibbons for $60 a month plus half the profits of the bar on the steamboat, which was commonly called the *Mouse* because it was less than one-fifth the size of the competing steamboats. In the summer of 1818, Vanderbilt began running the *Mouse* between New Jersey and the Battery in New York City. The new captain made improvements to the rickety boat, ran it on time and made a profit because it was cheap to operate. But when passengers complained about crowding, Vanderbilt had to lower the fares, eliminating most of the profit. As a result, only weeks after taking over the boat, Vanderbilt was able to persuade Gibbons to order a new, larger and more commodious boat, the *Bellona*, which was six times the tonnage of the *Mouse*. Built according to Vanderbilt's specifications and under his supervision, it was launched in 1818. He became its captain, leaving the *Mouse* to a subordinate.

When Vanderbilt would arrive in New York, the monopoly interests repeatedly tried to have him arrested, forcing the wily captain to come up with a series of evasive strategies. These included building a secret closet in the hold where he could hide before departure back to New Jersey. Pleased by his employee's resourcefulness, Gibbons raised his salary to $2,000 a season. Displeased by Vanderbilt's resourcefulness, the Livingston monopoly offered him a $5,000 annual salary to jump ship and run *Atalanta*, its largest boat on the Hudson. Vanderbilt demurred, preparing to remain independent with the idea of starting his own steamboat company in the future.[26]

In 1823, Vanderbilt got his first taste of steamboat ownership. After he designed the *Fanny* for Gibbons, the owner gave Vanderbilt one-third ownership in the vessel that eventually worked out of Boston.[27]

The Supreme Court's 1824 ruling in *Gibbons v. Ogden* that the New York monopoly violated the power of Congress to regulate interstate commerce brought a period of great expansion to the steamboat industry. The ruling meant that Vanderbilt could begin the company he had been dreaming of, but he decided to wait until he had accumulated more capital and to see what effect free competition would have on the industry.[28]

In preparation for operating his own company, Vanderbilt, while still working for Gibbons, designed and commissioned the construction of a medium-sized steamboat named the *Citizen* that was launched from New York in 1828. He operated it between New York and New Brunswick, New Jersey, on the Raritan River. He soon commenced a price war and, despite a thin profit margin, began offering free meals as an incentive.[29]

Vanderbilt ended up waiting five years after the Supreme Court ruling to go out on his own. In 1829, at age thirty-five, he finally established his own steamboat operation in combination with stage drivers in New Jersey. It was called the Dispatch Line. He would spend the next two decades expanding routes from New York through ruthless competition. He acquired from Gibbons the old *Bellona*, making his cousin John Vanderbilt its captain, and a smaller vessel he renamed *Emerald*. The *Citizen* and *Bellona* operated between Manhattan and Staten Island with Cornelius Vanderbilt serving as captain on the *Citizen*. Vanderbilt used the *Emerald* on a route along the Atlantic Ocean to the Delaware River.[30]

The price war with the competing Union Line on the New York to Philadelphia route that almost bankrupted both companies ended in 1830 with a deal for Vanderbilt to dissolve the Dispatch Line and leave the Raritan route to operate on the Hudson River. However, he did continue to operate boats from Elizabeth-Town (now Elizabeth), New Jersey, along the north shore of Staten Island and managed to make money on what had been an unprofitable route.[31]

Competition on the Hudson River was as intense as the battles for passengers on the New Jersey to New York routes. But Vanderbilt found an opening when the *General Jackson*, half-owned and operated by his brother Jacob between New York and Peekskill, exploded in the spring of 1831 near Haverstraw, probably because the steam escape valve was kept closed to increase speed. Fourteen people were killed immediately or subsequently from their injuries while others were scalded but survived.[32] The *General Jackson* was repaired and eventually went back into service.[33]

Boiler explosions were common in the era. In 1826, there were two explosions in Charleston, South Carolina, with four deaths. The following March, the *Oliver Ellsworth* experienced a boiler accident on the Sound near the Connecticut River, and the steam killed a fireman and injured several others.[34] Two years later, at least ten people died when the *Tricolor* exploded from a lack of water in its boiler near Wheeling, then part of Virginia. Several people were killed when the boiler on the *Macon* exploded in 1830 in Georgia.[35]

The 1831 *General Jackson* explosion created an opening for Vanderbilt's new boat *Cinderella*, launched in New York that year. The swift, narrow-beamed vessel did a thriving business and made a great deal of money for its owner. Vanderbilt used the profits to buy the other half interest in the *General Jackson* while it was being repaired so that he and Jacob could operate it together the next year.[36]

For a time, the Vanderbilts had the Peekskill–New York route to themselves, the first time Cornelius Vanderbilt found himself on the beneficial side of monopoly operation. But competition inevitably materialized. It came from Daniel Drew, who had started out as a cattle drover and then tavern manager in Manhattan. Over the next four decades, he would generally be a bitter rival to Vanderbilt, but there were periods when they were partners and friends. Drew formed a company to run the *Water Witch* between Peekskill and the city, getting financial backing from Putnam County farmers who believed they were being overcharged by the Vanderbilt brothers. Predictably, Vanderbilt and Drew engaged in a price war. With both men running out of money, a deal was reached for Drew to sell controlling interest in the *Water Witch* to Vanderbilt. He immediately pulled the vessel off the river route and returned his rates to their original level. Jacob Vanderbilt, commonly known as Captain Jake, later bought out his brother's interest in the *Water Witch* and ran it between Hartford, Connecticut, and New York.[37]

Again without competition on the Peekskill route, Cornelius Vanderbilt began looking to extend his operation to Albany to compete with the more established companies operating that far north. In anticipation of that expansion, he sold two of his oldest steamboats, including the *Bellona*, and used the money to build the *Westchester* in 1832. The largest vessel Vanderbilt had built, the speedy *Westchester* made its first trip to Albany in May. The established operators, running ten boats under the umbrella of the Hudson River Steamboat Association, initially ignored Vanderbilt, allowing him to make a substantial profit.[38]

But after the new Vanderbilt Line added the *Union*, built in 1833 by the New York shipyard of Bishop & Simonson (where his nephew Jeremiah Simonson was a partner), his competitors set out to sink the upstart interloper. They began slashing prices from three dollars to one dollar, to ten cents and eventually to zero. Vanderbilt matched them and apparently broke even by raising prices for meals and drinks. In order to gain customers, the captains did whatever they could to speed up trips and often raced their competitors by boosting the pressure in their boilers well beyond their design limits.[39]

The most brazen attempt to save time came if only a few passengers were getting off at a scheduled stop. They would be landed "on the fly." Customers would be placed in a small boat towed behind the steamer with a crew member aboard. When the vessel neared the landing, it would slow and veer toward shore and the crew member would steer the small craft toward the dock. "Passengers were expected to jump out before the line snapped the boat from under their feet, but often they were treated to an involuntary bath. Not until some years later, after several persons were drowned, did the Legislature forbid 'fly landings.'"[40]

Vanderbilt and his competitors on the Hudson shared a common belief. They watched with great interest as the first railroads were constructed and came to the same conclusion: that the new form of transportation could not compete with steamboats and would serve only to bring passengers to them. Although he eventually would become a railroad tycoon, initially, Vanderbilt developed a much more negative view of trains than the other steamboat operators. The reason likely stems from the fact that he was involved in the nation's first serious railroad accident—possibly on his first train trip—on November 8, 1833. He was traveling to Philadelphia on the Camden and Amboy Railroad at more than twenty-five miles an hour when an axle broke on the car in front of his and the car in which he was riding overturned. Vanderbilt was thrown out and down a thirty-foot embankment. While some passengers were killed, Vanderbilt suffered several broken ribs and a punctured lung. Although initially almost paralyzed by the pain, he did convalesce slowly.[41]

While recovering into early 1834, Vanderbilt designed and ordered two steamboats, *Champion* and *Nimrod*, selling two older vessels to pay for them. To distinguish his operation from the established lines, he renamed his company the People's Line so he could portray his competitors as greedy monopolists while he was their champion by driving down fares.[42]

At the end of the 1834 season, which had been marked by a new round of price warfare, the members of the Hudson River Steamboat Association once again decided the best way to deal with Vanderbilt was to buy him off. This time, Vanderbilt was receptive. Robert L. Stevens negotiated a deal for Vanderbilt to leave the Hudson for ten years in return for $100,000 as a bonus on top of an annual payment of $5,000. It was a high price, but it would pay off once the fares reverted to their old levels. Vanderbilt used the money to shift his operation to the growing and profitable routes on Long Island Sound.[43] He knew it because he had already owned sailing vessels that operated on that body of water.[44]

The routes on the Sound were attractive because traffic was continually increasing and railroads were working their way southwest from Boston to open new routes to a succession of coastal cities. Fares were high and

PEOPLE'S LINE.
ARRANGEMENT FOR APRIL.
Fare from Newport, $4.50, and found.

THE Steam-Boat Lex-
INGTON, Capt. Vander-
bilt, will leave New York
and Providence, as fol-
lows:—

Leaves Providence.	Leaves New York.
Wednesday, April 5	Monday, April 3
Saturday, 8	Thursday, 6
Wednesday, 12	Monday, 10
Saturday, 15	Thursday, 13
Wednesday, 19	Monday, 17
Saturday, 22	Thursday, 20
Wednesday, 26	Monday, 24
Saturday, 29	Thursday, 27

The Hour for leaving Providence is fixed
at 4 o'clock, on the arrival of the afternoon
cars—and New York at 5 P. M.

☞ The Lexington will arrive at New
York, in time for passengers to take the Philadelphia or Albany Boats on the same morning.

N. B.—Newport and New Bedford passengers can be accommodated with Berths in
this Boat, by applying the day previous to
her leaving.

For further information, enquire of H. E.
BREWSTER, Thames street, Newport.

April 13.

In 1834, to distinguish his operation from established steamboat lines, Cornelius Vanderbilt renamed his company the People's Line so he could portray his competitors as greedy monopolists. *Author photo.*

competition was scarce, except on the New York to Hartford route where Captain Jacob Vanderbilt was running his *Water Witch* using familiar family tactics by slashing the fare to one dollar from the usual eight. *Water Witch* quickly accumulated most of the traffic while crimping the profits of the previously dominant carrier on the route, Hartford Steamboat Company.[45]

While his brother was operating between Manhattan and Hartford, Vanderbilt was focused on the route between New York and Providence, Rhode Island, a thriving and growing commercial center. A group of prominent New Yorkers had organized the Boston & Providence Railroad, a forty-three-mile line that would link the two cities and allow passengers and freight going to and from Boston to connect to Long Island Sound steamboats without a voyage around Cape Cod. It was to be typical of New England's railroads in being short and designed to be part of a combined land-sea route between Boston and New York. The cost of building a railroad between those two cities was considered unaffordable with the capital available at the time, particularly because of all the rivers that would need to be bridged. In 1835, construction crews completed a four-year project working southwest from Boston. Their destination was the India Point dock in Providence, where trains could connect with steamboats operated by the Boston & New York Transportation Company, an association of shipowners later incorporated as the New Jersey Steam Navigation Company because that state was granting charters freely for enterprises outside its borders.[46] The stockholders of both companies were mostly the same people. The railroad-steamboat connection cemented the Transportation Company's near monopoly on steamboat traffic on the Sound.[47]

Journalist Benjamin Perly Poore later wrote that when the steamboats were waiting at India Point, "immense quantities of wood were piled up, for each boat consumed between thirty and forty cords on a trip through Long Island Sound." He added that there were "no staterooms, the passengers occupying berths, and at dinner and supper the captain of the boat occupied the head of the table, having seated near him any distinguished passengers."[48] There were no separate classes of tickets, so a banker could share the table with a tailor.[49]

Steamboating on Long Island Sound was more problematic than operating on the Hudson River or New York Harbor. The body of water, about one hundred miles long and up to twenty miles wide, could become extremely rough. And the currents and rocks at Hell Gate at its western end made navigation tricky. Fog was not unusual on the eastern ends of the runs. In winter, captains had to cope with freezing temperatures and floating ice. To deal with the conditions, boats for the Sound were built stronger and usually wider than those operating on the Hudson.

In 1834, to prepare to engage competitors out on open water, Vanderbilt began construction of the *Lexington*, a vessel that six years later would become the most notorious to ever sail on Long Island Sound.

3

CONSTRUCTION AND EARLY OPERATION OF THE *LEXINGTON*

Cornelius Vanderbilt spent freely in building the *Lexington* to be the fastest and most luxurious steamboat on Long Island Sound. To dominate the route between Providence and Boston, Vanderbilt turned again to Bishop & Simonson, which had constructed the *Union* for him in 1833. His nephew Jeremiah Simonson and Joseph Bishop had built a new shipyard in 1834 at the foot of Walnut Street in Manhattan.[50]

In the early nineteenth century, shipbuilders did not rely on blueprints. Instead, they carved a "half model" showing a side view of the vessel. When they were satisfied with the design, its outline would be transferred at full size to the shop floor so carpenters could measure and cut wood for assembly.

In the fall of 1834, Vanderbilt brought a half model of the *Lexington* to Bishop & Simonson's office downtown near Corlears Hook, south of today's Williamsburg Bridge. The two men, among New York's most experienced shipbuilders, had never seen a design like it. After seventeen years in the steamboat business and having built or owned about fifteen paddle-wheelers, Vanderbilt was proposing what one shipping expert described as "an entirely new class of steam vessels."[51]

After the sinking of the *Lexington*, Bishop testified at the inquest, whose findings were printed in two booklets, which are the sources for the testimony that follows.[52]

Bishop said, "We built her for Captain Cornelius Vanderbilt. His instructions were to make her as strong as possible. There was no written contract, no price agreed upon beforehand."[53]

The *Lexington* before the fire, by James and John Bard. *Public domain.*

The partners realized the steamboat would have to be very strong because their customer wanted the twin paddlewheels enlarged significantly over any previous design, to a diameter of twenty-four feet. Turning them would require a new engine design far more powerful than any ever installed in a steamboat. Vanderbilt envisioned a single huge engine that could perform the work of two conventional engines, saving as much as 50 percent on fuel.[54]

Vanderbilt's design called for the typical three decks: (1) a main deck over the hold where the steam engine was located, (2) a promenade deck on which would sit the wheelhouse where the pilot or crew member would steer and (3) an upper deck behind the wheelhouse that would protect cargo on the deck or passengers below from sparks or cinders from the smokestack. But Vanderbilt's design for the hull was far from conventional. He later commented that "her shape was very peculiar." The hull was unusually long and narrow and designed for speed. But because a long and narrow hull would typically "hog" or sag at the ends, Vanderbilt proposed to reinforce it by using a box-frame design with an arched deck based on plans for a bridge, rather than a vessel, he found in a publication titled *Town's Patent for Bridges*.[55]

Bishop testified at the inquest that

> *her floor timbers and futtocks* [curved timber ribs that reinforce the lower part of a hull] *were part oak and part chestnut; her floor timbers were 16 inches in width, and 6 inches in thickness; at amidships, they were about 6 inches apart; they would range from 6 to 16 inches; she was planked with oak; waist* [middle of the hull] *was pine. She was 205*

feet from stem to stern post; breadth of beam 22 feet; she was...fastened in the best manner....There was a great quantity of iron screw bolts used, more than was ever put in a boat of the description, before or since, that I have heard of. Her deck was white pine, two and a half inches thick, and five inches in width. She was about 46 feet across from outside to outside her [paddle]*guards....*

We always considered her a very strong boat. She had three kelsons [keelsons—structures running the length of a ship that fasten the transverse floorboards to the keel below] *and* [a lower] *bilge keelson besides; they were about 14 inches square. About the chimney there was all the precaution against fire usual.*

Vanderbilt decided to name his revolutionary steamboat *Lexington* after the place where another revolution had begun. The interior was lavish, with teak railings, paneling and stairways. Vanderbilt personally supervised the work. "My instructions in building the *Lexington* were given from day to day," Vanderbilt explained when he testified at the coroner's inquest.

All my boats were thus built under my directions. The Lexington *was built of first rate materials, chestnut, cedar, oak and white and yellow pine; she was fastened in what we thought the best manner—I think she had 30 per cent more fastenings than any other boat—as an evidence of her strength, she has navigated the Sound of four years, and never* [had to cancel a scheduled trip] *for the weather. I had so much confidence in her strength, that I always instructed my captains never to stop for foul weather, but if they could see to go ahead, to always go.*

The new steamboat was propelled by a wood-fueled vertical-beam—commonly called a walking beam—steam engine that was designed to allow the vessel to travel at almost twenty-nine miles an hour. The engine had a forty-eight-inch-diameter steam cylinder with an eleven-foot stroke. The piston rod connected to a shaft that drove the forward pivot on the walking beam, which converted the vertical motion to the horizontal shaft that powered a crank that turned the paddlewheels.[56] The 140-horsepower steam engine was fabricated by the West Point Foundry in Cold Spring, New York, on the east bank of the Hudson River opposite West Point.[57]

In building the *Lexington*, Vanderbilt placed a high priority on safety, which provided a marketing advantage in an age when boiler explosions, fires and other steamboat mishaps were common. The smokestack was encased as it

The West Point Foundry in Cold Spring on the Hudson River, which made the steam engine for the *Lexington*. *Courtesy of the Putnam History Museum.*

ran up through the decks, and he allowed no combustible materials to be placed near it, the boilers or steampipes. In order to avoid moving hot cinders around a wooden vessel, the steamboat was designed with a sixteen-inch-diameter pipe running down through the hull so debris from the boilers could be dumped directly into the water. The vessel was equipped with a portable "fire engine" pump with hoses. Two lifeboats were placed near the stern with a third forward on the promenade deck. As in the case with the *Titanic* in 1912, the lifeboats could accommodate only half the passengers and crew on a fully booked trip, but they met the statutory requirements at the time.[58]

The innovations built into the *Lexington* threatened the Boston & New York Transportation Company's dominance on the route between New York and Providence. As the sleek vessel was nearing completion, the company's directors decided to build a new steamboat, the *Massachusetts*, to compete with it. They sent their general agent, Captain William Comstock, a forty-eight-year-old veteran of the industry, to snoop around the shipyard to investigate the upstart competitor. He waited until the engine was installed and then slipped in for a quick look.[59]

Comstock was skeptical of the radical design, saying later, "I did not like her build." But he added, "I had no doubts of her strength and of the plan of securing her deck. In the structure of her keelsons, I think them stronger than any boat I ever saw." Comstock was so impressed that he went to the shipyard of Brown & Bell and had the design of the *Massachusetts* modified. That new boat would be the same length as the *Lexington* but far bigger—676 tons to 488—and he wanted it to be as strong and fast as Vanderbilt's design. That would prove hard to achieve.[60]

By the time *Lexington* was launched into the East River in April 1835, Vanderbilt had spent $75,000—the equivalent of about $2.5 million today—on it, but it proved to be an excellent investment. Comparing it to the Transportation Company's boats, Bishop remarked that "none of them are stronger than the *Lexington*." After helping to install the cylinder for the steam engine, engineer Theodosius F. Secor commented, "I consider her as perfect an engine as ever was built."[61]

Besides passengers, Vanderbilt had commissioned the *Lexington* primarily to carry a single commodity: cotton. In the 1830s, that fiber drove the American economy and dominated the nation's political environment. To meet the demand from British textile mills and increasingly mills in New England, cotton planters had expanded westward. Once the cotton was harvested, the crop enriched not only the planters but also the merchants, shippers and financiers in New York. Much of the cotton was shipped to Great Britain via Manhattan rather than directly from southern ports. A committee of southern legislators concluded that one-third of each dollar paid for cotton was spent in New York. Increasingly over time, more of the dirty white bales were unloaded from oceangoing ships on New York's docks and then reloaded onto vessels headed for the mills lining rivers in New England. Those first real factories in the United States wove fabric that often made its way back to New York to be made into clothing distributed by the city's merchants. "By the time the *Lexington* took shape in its shipyard, New York had emerged as capital of the commercial revolution, Boston as capital of the industrial," Vanderbilt biographer T.J. Stiles wrote. "Businessmen, craftsmen, and messengers, cargoes of cotton and kegs of gold, all passed between them in rising numbers. It was the aorta of the American economy."[62]

The Maiden Voyage

The *Lexington* was placed into service on June 1, 1835, with a crew of about thirty-five. On its first trip, with streamers flying, the vessel covered the 210 miles to Providence at an average record-setting speed of about 17 miles per hour. The Transportation Company's envious Captain Comstock watched the vessel surge up the East River at the astonishing speed of 20 miles per hour.[63]

The twelve-hour trip awed travelers who regularly spent eighteen hours or more on the route. "Fastest Boat in the World," announced the

Journal of Commerce. Though "elegantly fitted up," the paper commented, "her superiority is in her firmness and ease in the water, and above all, in her speed, in which we suppose it is safe to say, she surpasses any boat in the world, and has in fact reached a degree which was supposed two years ago impossible." The *Journal* voiced a broad consensus that Vanderbilt had achieved one of the great technical triumphs of the day. "Her construction exhibits great knowledge of mechanical principles, and a peculiarly bold and independent genius."[64]

In 1835, the Transportation Company operated six steamboats on the Sound: the relatively small *Boston*, *Providence*, *President*, *Benjamin Franklin* and *Rhode Island* and the massive new *Massachusetts*. Before Vanderbilt inserted himself, the company's monopoly on the route enabled it to charge passengers eight dollars a trip.[65]

On June 15, two weeks after the *Lexington*'s maiden voyage, the Boston & Providence Railroad began service. Because of the overlapping owners, it promptly gave the Transportation Company exclusive rights to land at the railroad dock in Providence, and the companies established coordinated fares and schedules. The contract was signed by Charles H. Russell, president of the steamboat company, and William W. Woolsey, president of the railroad. Both men were directors of both companies. Comstock would say that the Transportation Company had "done up" Cornelius Vanderbilt.[66]

But he spoke too soon. Vanderbilt prospered by attracting freight from factories in and around Providence, but he was more concerned about attracting passengers—the most lucrative part of the trade. And to attract passengers, a steamboat needed to be faster than the competition. The *Lexington* was. And to further undermine his competitors, Vanderbilt slashed the fare, once as high as ten dollars, to three dollars, and he adjusted his schedule to dock in Providence so his customers could walk to the railroad station in time to buy tickets for the Boston train. Passenger Philip Hone wrote in his diary about the trip from New York that "the time [for the train ride] was 2 hours and a half, and the *Lexington* steam boat goes from New York to Providence in 12 hours, so that persons leaving this city at 6 in the morning can unstrap their trunks at their lodgings in Boston by daylight on a summer day."[67]

While Cornelius Vanderbilt was at the helm for the maiden voyage and early runs, he soon summoned his brother Jacob to take over. Captain Jake hired another captain to run the *Water Witch* on the Hartford–New York route.[68]

Thanks to the low fare and *Lexington*'s speed and comfort, the new steamboat proved to be an immediate success. "She did an excellent business from the beginning, but to attract full loads sometimes an excursion rate

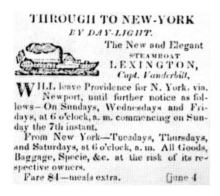

THROUGH TO NEW-YORK
BY DAY-LIGHT.

The New and Elegant **STEAMBOAT** L E X I N G T O N, *Capt. Vanderbilt,*

WILL leave Providence for N. York, via. Newport, until further notice as follows—On Sundays, Wednesdays and Fridays, at 6 o'clock, a. m. commencing on Sunday the 7th instant.

From New York—Tuesdays, Thursdays, and Saturdays, at 6 o'clock, a. m. All Goods, Baggage, Specie, &c. at the risk of its respective owners.

Fare $4—meals extra.   [June 4

A newspaper advertisement for the *Lexington* from June 1835.

of a round-trip for the regular [one-way] fare was granted," biographer Lane wrote. "Apparently the number of passengers would have been even larger but for the reputation which Captain Jake was acquiring for the bold and dangerous way he drove the vessels under his command. The owners of a rival vessel advertised that their steamer would 'leave five minutes after the *Lexington* to prevent the reckless destruction of property and to protect the passengers.' Apparently Jake, with his staunch ship under him, welcomed the occasional collision."[69]

The lower fares made steamboat travel on Long Island Sound widely accessible in the 1830s. The paddle-wheeler travel experience was chronicled in newspapers and books of the time. Charles Dickens wrote about a trip on a Sound steamboat in the late 1830s:

> *Directly you have left the wharf,* [and] *all the life, and stir, and bustle… cease. The passengers, unless the weather be very fine indeed, usually congregate below.…There is always a clerk's office on the lower deck, where you pay your fare; a ladies' cabin; baggage and stowage rooms; engineer's room; and in short a great variety of perplexities which render the discovery of the gentleman's cabin a matter of some difficulty. It often occupies the whole length of the boat…and has three or four tiers of berths* [bunks] *on each side.*

During the day, the crew set up two rows of long rectangular tables where stewards served drinks and elaborate meals.[70]

As steamboat travel became more and more common, customers demanded higher speed and more comfort. "Passengers are now-a-days expected to have every thing extravagant," Captain Comstock grumbled.[71] To better accommodate passengers on the overnight trips, berths were added on the *Lexington* over the winter of 1836–37.[72]

Vanderbilt took a macro strategic view of the battle for control of Long Island Sound transportation. In the fall of 1835, he shifted the *Lexington* to the New York–Hartford route to take on Menemon Sanford, another hardened steamboat captain who had dominated shipping to New Haven and Hartford. Sanford had a nasty reputation. "I believe him to be a person void of truth and character," Comstock wrote. Vanderbilt, who also despised Sanford, began an advertising offensive with headlines such as "OPPOSITION TO IMPOSITION: NO MONOPOLY—FREE TRADE & EQUAL RIGHTS." Fighting for market share on the Connecticut and Rhode Island routes, Vanderbilt began to concentrate all of his attention and resources on Long Island Sound. On August 27, 1835, he sold the *Water Witch*, *Cinderella* and his profitable New York Harbor ferry to a group of six men for the sizable sum of $74,000. That was enough to build the *Cleopatra*, another fast and luxurious steamboat modeled on the *Lexington*.[73]

In 1836, Vanderbilt rerouted the *Lexington* back to Providence under the command of brother Jacob. That prompted a response from the Transportation Company's chairman, Moses H. Grinnell, a New York maritime shipping merchant and Whig politician in his early thirties who shared with Vanderbilt having been poor in early life. To compete with the *Lexington*, Grinnell, who was also a commodore of the New York Yacht Club, ordered the *Rhode Island*, the *Massachusetts* and the *Narragansett*. All were bigger than the *Lexington* but could not match its speed. The *Narragansett* proved to be neither as fast nor as economical as Vanderbilt's steamboat and much less stable as well. While the *Narragansett* was relatively fast, it tended to pitch and roll even in small waves. That problem was compounded by the hull not being built strong enough to accommodate the vibrations of the large steam engine, which resulted in *Narraganset* spending much time in dry dock for recaulking between the planks.[74]

Vanderbilt responded to the added competition as he had always done. He reduced his fares even lower, eventually down to one dollar. Although he did this to sink his competitor with the goal of establishing his own monopoly, the *New York Evening Post* of February 18, 1837, focused on the savings to travelers and without a glance at Vanderbilt's history praised him as "the greatest practical anti-monopolist in the country."[75] That year, Vanderbilt added *Cleopatra* on an alternating schedule with *Lexington* so he now had a boat leaving each port every day.

The fact that none of the competing steamboats could outrun the *Lexington* was not overlooked by the newspapers and the public. "The speed and excellence of this boat require no comment from us," the *Providence Courier* noted. The newspaper described Vanderbilt's boat as "this far-famed water witch, which measures distances as fast as one can keep account of the miles." Comstock conceded that the *Lexington* was "the fastest boat on the route."[76]

A receipt for shipping cargo on the *Lexington* in 1836. *Tod Thonger collection.*

Not everyone was a fan of the *Lexington* and its owner. The *New-York Mirror* wrote, "Mr. Vanderbilt, a large capitalist, and doubtless an enterprising man, with a view of breaking down what has been denominated by the 'odious eastern monopoly' has placed several swift and commodious steamers on the Boston line, and you may now take a trip from New-York to Providence for the trifling consideration of one dollar, lawful currency!"[77] But the newspaper added that the benefit of cheap and fast transportation provided by Vanderbilt could destroy the established Transportation Company and foster an anarchic world without social distinctions. "In a crowded steamer…whose deck and cabin are thronged with what the great bard calls 'all sorts of people,'" the *Mirror* grumbled, "there is no more comfort than there is said to be in a badly governed family…when, the old ballad tells us, all is topsy-turvy."[78]

Vanderbilt scored a victory over the Transportation Company in 1837 when the Rhode Island legislature rejected an attempt by the Boston & Providence Railroad to block Vanderbilt from using the wharfs at the India Point depot. While the Transportation Company still held an exclusive contract with the railroad, during the winter of 1836–37 Vanderbilt's agent in Providence managed to convince the legislature that the contract violated the railroad's state charter, which specified fair and equal access to all steamboats making connections with the trains. The decision gave Vanderbilt space at the depot and his passengers the same access to the trains as his competitor. With the access assured, Vanderbilt added new vessels to take on other competitors and expand his route system. He began running the *Cleopatra* or the *Clifton* from New York to the end of the North Fork on Long Island and to Sag Harbor, locations previously reachable only by small sailing vessels or stagecoaches. He also expanded outside of the New York

Left: "Commodore" Cornelius Vanderbilt photographed late in life. *Library of Congress.*

Right: Statue of Cornelius Vanderbilt in front of Grand Central Terminal in Manhattan. He made his first fortune in steamboats before shifting his attention to monopolizing railroads in the region. *Author photo.*

region by establishing the elegant steam packet *North Carolina* on a route from New York to Wilmington, North Carolina, and Charleston, South Carolina. In reporting on the development, the *Norfolk Herald* was one of the first newspapers to bestow on Vanderbilt the honorific title "Commodore." The *Journal of Commerce* also began to call Vanderbilt the Commodore in 1837, and different historians credit each publication with being the first. Then the highest rank in the U.S. Navy, the title had also been given to notable steamboat men in the past.[79]

Meanwhile, Jacob Vanderbilt's reputation as an excellent, although sometimes reckless, captain was burnished in December 1837 when he brought the *Lexington* through a severe storm that snapped the tiller ropes leading to the rudder. The monthly *Ladies Companion* later described him as a man of "unsurpassed energy and decision of character, wonderful quickness, and reach of judgment and imperturbable calmness and resolution in the moment of danger."[80]

When the Boston & Providence extended its tracks southwest forty-eight miles to Stonington, Connecticut, in 1837, the established steamboats began running there as well as Providence. The trip was faster, but passengers arrived at Stonington to transfer to the train at three o'clock in the morning, a cause of much grumbling.[81]

With the improved service options, passenger demand filled all of the boats owned by both companies. That prompted Vanderbilt and Grinnell to cash in, with each raising the fare back to eight dollars per trip for the Providence run. So much for Vanderbilt being "the greatest practical anti-monopolist in the country." The fare between New York and Stonington was set at six dollars, and the railroad ticket between Boston and Stonington was only one dollar more than the fare between Boston and Providence. With this price structure and the higher speed on the rails, business leaders in Providence rightly became concerned that travelers would stop connecting through their city. In addition, transferring from steamboat to train farther west eliminated the rough passage around Point Judith at the mouth of Narragansett Bay. In response, investors in Providence formed the Atlantic Steamboat Company in 1837. A year later, they launched the *John W. Richmond*, a five-hundred-ton vessel named for the company president.[82]

The *Richmond* was designed to beat every other steamboat on the Sound and return Providence to its preeminent role. It competed directly with the Transportation Company's *Narragansett* and consistently outpaced it. Rather than build a faster steamboat, the Transportation Company opted to offer Vanderbilt $60,000 for the *Lexington* if it could beat the *Richmond*. Vanderbilt accepted the challenge.[83]

In the widely publicized race in the spring of 1838, shortly after the *Richmond* was launched, that vessel was commanded by Captain William H. Townsend, considered one of the best skippers on the Sound and the man who had overseen construction of the steamboat. Jake Vanderbilt, "whose reputation for daring deeds with a steamboat has been equaled by few," was at the helm of the *Lexington*.[84]

On race day, the *Richmond* steamed into Stonington from Newport, where it had docked overnight. The *Lexington* arrived from New York to meet the Boston train, and soon thereafter both vessels left for New York. The *Richmond* took an early lead. A newspaper reporter describes what happened next:

> *For ten or a dozen miles down the Sound there was no perceptible change in the relative position of the boats. Then dense clouds of smoke poured from* Lexington, *a sheet of flame shot up from her stack, her wheels*

turned swifter, and a cheer burst from passengers as they realized the gap between them and Richmond *was closing. It was an anxious moment on board* Richmond *for* Lexington *was gaining fast. Where was Captain Townsend? There was no reply. He was not to be found. But the movements on board* Lexington *had not escaped his eye. The moment that the boat left Stonington men had been set picking out the most resinous wood* [that burned hotter] *and piling it for immediate use. The engineer had been tightening bolts and screws, and* Richmond *was ready for the race.*

At the first puffs of black smoke from Lexington, *Captain Townsend had rushed to the engine room and was consulting the engineer. "Oh, she can stand considerably more," said that functionary; and the Captain answered, "Well, put in the fat wood and let her go." She did go. Volumes of smoke poured from her funnel, and the roar of her fires could be heard all over the boat. A column of flame stood a pillar of fire above her. She trembled at every revolution of her wheels. The water seethed and boiled beneath her, fire and smoke were around about her overhead. She advanced like the rush of an avalanche—she was a moving volcano. Slowly, steadily, she moved away from* Lexington; *wider and wider grew the interval between them, until at last* Richmond *dashed between the rocks at Hail Gate and* Lexington *was seen no more until she came by an hour after* Richmond *had made fast to her pier.*

Vanderbilt never forgave Richmond *for that day's work.* Lexington *was, without doubt, the faster boat, but* Richmond *had fairly beaten her once and nobody could say that she was unable to do it again.*[85]

Losing the race did nothing to diminish the appeal of the *Lexington*. And while it remained a moneymaker for Vanderbilt, he was always receptive to a good deal and always looking to upgrade his fleet. He also liked to keep the pressure up on his competitors. In July 1838, the Commodore ran a newspaper ad in which he crowed about his "20 years experience in steamboats." He added that "it has been my whole study, and I have built and owned some twenty, and can say, without any intention of boasting, that not one life has ever been lost in any of the number."[86]

Vanderbilt biographer T.J. Stiles describes the Commodore's aggressive method of competition:

Vanderbilt battered his opponents with his grasp of both tactics and strategy….He was better capitalized than his opponents, which enabled him to absorb losses. But he could also make money even in fare wars

FIFTY CENTS to PROVIDENCE!—The Lexington, it is said is going on the Boston and New York route, to take Passengers from New York to Providence for 50 cents!

"FARE REDUCED."—NO MONOPOLY.—*Peoples' New Line for Boston, via Newport and Providence.*—Cabin passage one dollar—Deck fifty cents.—The steamer LEXINGTON, Capt. Vanderbilt, will leave New York for Newport and Providence, on Saturday, the 4th inst., at 5 o'clock, P. M, from Pier No. 4 North River. Freight taken at 4 cents per foot. For further information apply on board.

The engine, boilers and hull of the above boat have been put in complete order, and *the public may rest assured that there will be no racing practiced.* It being entirely unnecessary to sustain her well established reputation for speed. The regular days for the Lexington to leave New York will be Wednesdays and Saturdays, until further notice.   a4 3m

Top: The *Long Island Star* reported on Vanderbilt slashing the price of a ticket for the *Lexington* to fifty cents.

Bottom: An advertisement in the New York *Morning Herald* reports on Vanderbilt lowering his fare to fifty cents for riding on deck and one dollar to travel in the cabin.

> *in which he slashed his one-way ticket price as low as fifty cents, thanks to his ability to control costs. This was a result, in part, of a technical advantage: the* Lexington*'s engine and hull design had saved an estimated fifty percent in fuel expenses, by far the largest operating cost, and all his later boats followed its plan. He kept personnel expenses down by shifting them to his customers; passengers began to complain that they were expected to tip for almost everything.*

Comstock lamented in letters that Vanderbilt outmatched his company in everything from pricing to renting office space to distributing handbills.[87]

In the middle of a fare war, despite *Lexington* having lost the highly publicized race, Vanderbilt approached Robert Schuyler, president of the Transportation Company. He said if his competitor did not buy the *Lexington*, which he now considered too small to operate profitably, he would run it to Providence with a fare of only one dollar. Even adding the cost of the ticket for the Boston & Providence Railroad, this would allow travelers to move from New York to Boston for less than the five dollars charged by

☞ An accredited report is prevalent that the Transportation (*monopoly*) Company has purchased the old steamboat Lexington, and intend to run her in opposition to the Richmond during the coming season. Passengers who value their comfort will avoid her, we think.

On January 16, 1839, the *Rhode Island Republican* reported the sale of the *Lexington* by Cornelius Vanderbilt.

his competitor. Schuyler realized the potential losses could be ruinous and began negotiating with Vanderbilt.[88]

In December 1838, the Transportation Company agreed to pay $60,000 for the *Lexington*. One banker estimated the value of the vessel at half that amount, saying the rest was basically a bribe to keep Vanderbilt from competing. "We found it unprofitable [to fight with Vanderbilt] and concluded that it was better to be at peace than at war, on any terms," Comstock explained. The company asked Vanderbilt to provide a written pledge that he would never again interfere with it. Vanderbilt refused, stating that the company could rely on his verbal assurances. Comstock commented that he had "no confidence in him keeping his word" and assumed the Commodore would again torment the company.[89]

After buying the *Lexington,* the Transportation Company further squelched competition by acquiring a controlling interest in the *Richmond* and placing it on routes serving northern New England.[90]

After the renamed New Jersey Steam Navigation and Transportation Company purchased the *Lexington* for $60,000, the company invested another $12,000 to refurbish the interior and convert the steam engine to burn coal. Fans were added to force more air into the fireboxes to increase the heat and speed of the vessel. The company's general agent, Captain William Comstock, described the renovations: "The grate-bars were raised up eighteen inches, the flues contracted, and the insides of the furnaces were filled with fire brick and iron pans that always had water in them, and the whole width of the boiler at the after end was filled up with brick and iron."[91]

Vanderbilt's younger brother and Staten Island neighbor Jacob agreed to continue running the *Lexington* for the Transportation Company and managed the reconstruction project for Comstock.[92]

The new owner of the *Lexington* would not be able to replicate Cornelius Vanderbilt's safety record. The Transportation Company would not be able to brag that "not one life has ever been lost."

4

THE LAST VOYAGE

After spending $72,000 to buy and overhaul the *Lexington*, the New Jersey Steam Navigation and Transportation Company would get to operate the famous steamboat for only a year.

On Monday, January 13, 1840, after boarding passengers and loading cargo, including nearly 150 bales of cotton placed on the main deck, the revolutionary vessel designed by Cornelius Vanderbilt eased away from the company pier at the Battery in Manhattan at 4:00 p.m. The temperature was four degrees, and during that night, "the thermometer marked nineteen degrees below zero—a temperature unknown in that place before or since," according to an account published in 1887.[93] The cold spell had left sheets of ice floating on Long Island Sound.

There had been trouble with the blowers on the steam engine on the last trip from Stonington, so the *Lexington* had been undergoing repairs at the pier. The steamboat had been expected to sail on Tuesday, January 14, but with the accumulation of ice on the waterways, it was decided to use the *Lexington* instead of another boat on Monday evening because of its strong construction. Because of the change, some of the regular crew remained at home in Providence. The clerk of the vessel, T.C. Gladding, was one of them.[94]

Also not aboard was Jacob Vanderbilt, still the regular captain of the *Lexington* after its sale by his brother, because he was home in bed with a head cold. The company replaced him with another of its captains, George Child, thirty-six, of Stonington, the youngest of ten children, who followed in his father's footsteps by becoming a captain.[95] Child, after running scheduled packet boats for several years, had four years' experience commanding steamboats on Long Island Sound for the Transportation Company. He usually ran the company's *Providence* or *Narragansett*.[96]

"George Child was a cautious skipper who rarely took chances," wrote author Clive Cussler, who put together the team that rediscovered the wreck of the *Lexington* in 1983.[97] He added that "most captains of the passenger boats plying the Sound were not comfortable mingling with the passengers and remained aloof in the wheelhouse or their cabins during most of the trip. But George Child was a warm and friendly man. He felt it was his duty to show courtesy to his passengers and reassure any, and there were a fair number, who were fearful of traveling on a steamboat."[98]

Even with the fare wars between the Transportation Company and Vanderbilt on hiatus, the more than one hundred passengers paid only one dollar, with meals extra, to travel in the salon. They could have paid half of that to ride on deck, but there were no takers on that frigid night.[99] They came primarily from New York City, Providence and Boston, with others from around New England, Pennsylvania, Baltimore and one even from England, according to the passenger list. A crew of thirty-four ran the boat and took care of passenger needs. The serving of refreshments was supervised by headwaiter Job Sand, who was white. The five waiters were Black, as was chambermaid Susan Holcomb. The passenger and crew list notes them as "Colored." The name of the head cook, Joseph Robinson, also Black, was on the crew list that was published, but it was later reported that he was home sick and was replaced by the second cook, Oliver Howell, also Black, while Isaac Pitman, a Black waiter, filled in for Howell.

The list of passengers included two prominent comedic actors from Boston. One was Charles L. Eberle, the father of three young children. His wife, Rachel, would give birth three months after his death to a fourth, Eugene A., who became an acclaimed Broadway actor.[100] The other actor, Henry J. Finn, who was also a playwright, had twelve children with his wife, Elizabeth Powell, a Boston actress, and was on his way to their summer home in Newport, Rhode Island.[101] Charles Follen was a professor of German literature at Harvard College and a minister. There were many parents with children, including Mrs. Russell Jarvis (whose first name was not recorded), described as a woman of rare beauty, who was traveling with two young daughters. William Townsend was giving his wife a break by taking their two girls on a vacation to Boston. Mary Russell had been married the day before in New York and was returning to her New England home without her new spouse to break the news to her parents. She would be a wife for one day. Not all the passengers were there for happy reasons. Three members of the family of recently deceased Henry A. Winslow, including his widow, Alice, were accompanying his coffin stowed in the hold for burial in Providence.[102]

Many were traveling for business, including Robert Blake, president of Wrentham Bank in Wrentham, Massachusetts; Abraham Howard of the Boston firm of Howard & Mersay; Captain William Greene of Providence, agent for the Minot Shoe Company of Maine; Samuel Henry from Manchester, England, from the firm of S.&A. Henry; and John Lemist, treasurer of the Boston Leather Company. Adolphus Harnden of Harnden's Express was the younger brother of William Frederick Harnden, founder of a nineteenth-century forerunner of FedEx. He was transporting gold coins amounting to $14,000 and silver coins amounting to $11,000 for the Merchants' Bank in Boston.[103]

Memorial stone for members of the Winslow family at the Grove Hill Cemetery in Waltham, Massachusetts. *Lexington* victim Alice B. Winslow is included with her siblings. *Tod Thonger photo.*

There were also several ship captains traveling as passengers: J.D. Carver; E.J. Kimball; David McFarland; John Mattison; Theophilus Smith; Benjamin Foster, who was returning from a three-year voyage to India; and twenty-four-year-old Chester Hillard, who would play a critical role in the events that followed.[104] (His name is spelled Hilliard in the contemporary accounts and in the censuses of 1850 and 1860 but Hillard on his gravestone.) Thanks to his calmness in the face of calamity, Hillard, captain of oceangoing cargo sailing ships, would be the only passenger to survive.

According to an account in the *Connecticut Courant* on February 1, dinner was served at 6:00 p.m. Oliver Howell and Isaac Pitman had prepared a choice of mutton with boiled tomatoes and baked flounder in wine sauce with rice. Hillard remembered two tables had been set that ran more than half the length of the cabin, with stoves in the center providing relief from the chill outside. It would be the last meal for all of those serving and eating except Hillard.

The Fire

Stephen Manchester

Stephen Manchester, the pilot, was steering the steamboat when the fire was discovered. One of three surviving crew members, the Providence, Rhode Island resident was a witness at the seventh day of the inquest into the disaster.

Manchester testified that he

> *was in the wheel house when…about 7:30 o'clock, someone came to the wheel house door and told me the boat was on fire; I don't know who it was.…My wheelman* [later said to be First Mate Edward Thurber or helmsman Martin Johnson] *was in the house with me; my first movement was to step out of the wheel-house and look aft; saw the upper deck burning all around the smoke pipe, blazing up two or three feet; the flame appeared to be in a thin sheet all around the smoke pipe, coming up through the promenade deck. I returned into the wheel-house and put the wheel hard-a-port to steer the boat for the land.* [With the vessel heading east, he likely steered to starboard, or right, to head for the Long Island shore and either misspoke at the inquest or the authors of the inquest transcript erred. The closest land was the Eatons Neck peninsula north of Huntington in western Suffolk County.] *I then thought it was very doubtful whether the fire could be extinguished. We were then about fifty miles to the east of this* [New York City], *and about four miles from the Long Island shore; at the rate we were then going, it would take us about twenty minutes to go to shore; from the way she was heading it might have taken three or four minutes to turn her. The highest* [he probably said or meant nearest] *land to us bore about south.*
>
> *We had not yet headed to the land, when something gave way, which I believe was the tiller rope.…Captain Child then came into the wheel-house and put his hand to the spoke of the wheel, and as he did so, the rope gave way…and at the same time the smoke came into the wheel house, and he was obliged to go out, and I went out too. I suspect he went aft, but I never saw him afterwards.…I then called to them on the forecastle* [by the bow] *to get out the fire engine and buckets; the engine was got out, but they could not get at the buckets, or at least I only saw a few. I am of the opinion the wheel ropes burnt off, but I could not have stood it longer even if there had been chains around the wheel.*

Manchester believed the *Lexington* had a backup steering apparatus by the stern with chains attached to the tiller and rudder because all steamboats were rigged that way. But he added, "I did not go aft to it, because I thought my services would be more useful forward."

> *After calling to get out the* [fire] *engine, I went to the life boat, and found some persons taking the tarpaulin off it.…I caught hold of the lashing of the boat, and requested them not to let her go until we got a line fastened to her. I called to those at the forecastle* [on the deck below] *to pass a line to make fast to her, which they did, and we fastened it to her bow. I think I called to them to make it fast to prevent the life boat going under the* [paddle]*wheel, and it was made fast. The fire was then burning through the promenade deck. I cut the lashing, and told them to launch the boat. I jumped from the promenade deck down to the forward deck, took hold of the hawser* [the rope attached to the bow of the lifeboat], *and found it was not fastened to the steamboat. I told them to hold on to the rope, but they all let go one after another; the engine was still going, and I was obliged to let go myself also; among those who held it were some of the waiters and passengers. We then found two buckets and commenced throwing water with them and the* [emptied] *species* [coin] *boxes; we got the water from over the side of the boat, which was then pretty much stopt; while doing this some others took the flagstaffs and parts of the bulwarks and made a raft, to which we made a line fast and hove it over the side of the boat; we then threw the baggage overboard from four baggage cars, and made them fast with a line; the engine was then entirely stopped; it worked from ten to fifteen minutes and kept working gradually slower until it stopped; we threw out every thing by which we thought any person could save themselves; we continued throwing on water in hopes that some person might come to our relief.*
>
> *The main deck now fell in as far as the capstan* [a large winch near the bow]*; the people had by this time got overboard, some of them drowned, and others hurrying onto the baggage cars, the raft and other things. What was left of the main deck was now on fire, and got us cornered up in so small a space that we could do nothing more by throwing water. There were then only eight or ten persons astern on the steamboat, and about 30 on the forecastle. They were asking me what they should do, and I told them I saw no chance for any of us; that if we stayed there, we should be burnt to death, and if we went overboard we should probably perish. Among those who were there were Mr. Hoyt and Van Cott, another person named Harnden…of the express line.*[105]

AWFUL CONFLAGRATION
OF THE STEAM BOAT **LEXINGTON** IN LONG ISLAND SOUND.

Lithograph of the burning *Lexington* by an anonymous artist. *Tod Thonger collection.*

For those on board, going over the side into the frigid water did not seem like a great option, particularly since fewer than 10 percent of the population at the time knew how to swim.[106] But it was better than burning to death.

Chester Hillard

When he boarded the *Lexington* at three o'clock, Captain Chester Hillard testified at the inquest, he "paid no particular attention" to the loading of the freight. "I think the greatest proportion of the freight consisted of cotton; it was stowed under the promenade deck." By the wheelhouse, "there was sufficient space for a person to pass" by the cotton bales. As he walked around the vessel, he noticed a lifeboat on the starboard side of the promenade deck forward of the wheelhouse and added that he did not pay attention to the two other lifeboats on either side toward the stern until they were being lowered during the fire.[107]

Hillard ate supper about six o'clock. The tables were filled, so some of the passengers had to wait for a second seating. Noting that he did not know Captain Child, he could not say if the vessel's master was dining with the passengers. When Hillard finished eating after thirty to forty-five minutes, he returned to his berth on the starboard side of the cabin.

"It was about an hour after supper that I heard the alarm of fire," Hillard testified. "I was then on the point of turning in. I had my coat and boots off.…I did not at the time apprehend any thing serious. I slipped on my coat and boots and went on deck. I put on my hat and took my overcoat on my arm. When I got on deck I discovered the casing of the smoke pipe on fire, and I think a part of the promenade deck was also on fire. There was a great rush of the passengers, and much confusion.…The after part of the casing was burning, and the fire was making aft. I thought at the time that the fire might be subdued." Hillard also noticed flames on the main deck below the promenade deck. The surviving passenger did not see Captain Child. He could hear crew members forward of him and thought they were trying to start the fire engine pump. He did not see anyone using the fire buckets.

Moving up to the promenade deck, Hillard saw that one of the two lifeboats had been filled by panicked passengers. Crew members were in the process of lowering it—despite the ship still forging ahead at thirteen miles per hour, making it virtually impossible to launch them successfully because the rushing water would inevitably flood and capsize them.

"They seemed to be stupidly determined to destroy themselves, as well as the boats which were their only means of safety," Hillard stated. "I went to the starboard boat, which they were lowering away; they lowered it until she took the water, and then I saw some one cut away the forward takle [block and tackle for lowering the lifeboat].…The boat instantly filled with water, there being at the time some twenty persons in her; the boat passed immediately astern." He went to the port side of the vessel and watched as the other boat full of passengers was lowered, filled with seawater and then drifted astern.

The experienced mariner had concluded by this point that the *Lexington* was doomed and the only question was whether any of those onboard could be saved. "I thought that the best thing that could be done was to run the boat ashore, and for this purpose went to the wheel-house to look for Captain Child.…I advised him to run for the shore. The Captain replied that she was already headed for the land. The fire by this time began to come up around the promenade deck, and the wheel-house was completely filled with smoke."

The witness testified that he saw two or three persons, including pilot Manchester, near the wheelhouse on the promenade deck working on the lifeboat stored there. "I was at this time apprehensive that the promenade deck would fall through. The life boat was cleared away. I assisted stripping off the canvas, but I had no notion of going in her." Hillard concluded that if the lifeboat was lowered to the main deck, filled with passengers and then put over the side while the vessel was still moving, it would swamp just like the other two boats. Nonetheless, "they cleared her away and I think launched her over the side."

With flames burning up through the promenade deck, Hillard testified, "I thought it was time for me to leave…. I then went aft and down on to the main deck. They were then at work with the hose, but whether by the aid of the [fire] engine, or not, I cannot say….The smoke was so dense that I could not see distinctly what they were about. I think that the communication with the fore part of the boat was by that time cut off."

It was now about twenty minutes after the first alarm of fire had been sounded and five minutes since the engine had stopped. Hillard added,

> *I then recommended to the few deck hands and passengers who remained, to throw the cotton overboard. This was done, myself lending my aid. I told the passengers that they must do something for themselves and the best*

A burning *Lexington* illustration by Fred Erving Dayton published in 1915. *From* Steamboat Days *by John Walcott Adams.*

thing they could do was to take to the cotton. There were perhaps ten or a dozen bales thrown overboard, which was pretty much all there was on the larboard [port or left] side which had not taken fire. I then cut off a piece of line, perhaps four or five fathoms [twenty-four to thirty feet], and with it spanned a bale of cotton, which I believe was the last one not on fire. It was a very snug square bale: It was about four feet long and three feet wide; and a foot and a half thick.

Charles Buckingham Smith

A watch owned by the *Lexington*'s captain, George Child. He did not have it with him when he died trying to launch a lifeboat. *Connecticut Historical Society.*

Charles Buckingham Smith of Norwich, Connecticut, one of the four firemen stoking the boilers, testified at the inquest that "the first time I heard the alarm of fire, was about 7:30 o'clock in the evening." Smith said he was asleep in his room above one of the paddlewheel guards when "coal heaver" Henry Reed came in and woke him. Reed told him that "the boat was all on fire." Smith testified, "I got out of my berth; the door of the room was open, directly opposite the steam chimney, and I saw the promenade deck and part of the casing around the chimney on fire."

He rushed to where the firehose was located and opened the valve. But the flames kept him away from the nozzle end of the hose, so it was useless.

I went aft…to get breath, then I tried to get the buckets down…which the fire prevented me from doing; then I went aft with the intention of getting into the boat, when I got aft I saw Captain Child standing on the rail, by the…boat, on the starboard side, and heard him sing out for the engineer. The engineer answered, the captain asked him if he could stop the engine; he replied it was impossible, as the fire prevented, and then I got to where Captain Child stood and saw the bow tackle of the boat cut away, with the boat full of passengers—the bows of the boat filled with water, and she swung round on her stern tackle. Captain Child sung out, hold onto the boat.

Child slipped down into the stern of the lifeboat, and Smith followed him. Just as he regained his footing, "the stern tackle was let go, but whether it was cut or not I don't know. That was the last I saw of the boat or captain. Captain Child was in the boat at the time."[108]

David Crowley

Second Mate David Crowley, the fourth and last man rescued, did not testify at the inquest because of the precarious state of his health, but he did provide accounts to the newspapers, one of which follows. He said that after hearing the alarm of fire, he ran to the smokestack on the main deck.

> *There* [he] *discovered six bales of cotton on fire, which had not then spread to any part of the wood-work. He immediately handed up to Captain Manchester, who was then on the promenade-deck, three pails of water, and then with the deck hands and waiters, continued to draw water and throw it on the fire; they did so without any confusion, and with the most strenuous exertion, until they were driven away by the strength of the flames. Captain Child was among them, aiding and directing, and it was not until all hopes of saving the boat was gone, that Captain Child, in reply to an inquiry from some of the passengers of what was to be done, replied, in a collected manner, "Gentlemen, take to the boats," and then went aft, himself; which was the last time Mr. Crowley saw him. He also stated that before leaving the wreck, he saw some of the quarter-boats launched by some of the passengers, and called out to them to put the* [drain] *plug in the boat; that he assisted one of the passages to throw overboard the hawser* [a heavy rope] *tub, and another, the chaffing board* [probably a fender board to prevent chafing of dock lines]*; that he himself at last threw over a side-plank* [possibly a gangplank or gangway]*, and jumped on it; soon afterward, swam to a bale of cotton which floated near him.*[109]

The Rescuers

The towering flames from the burning *Lexington* were visible from the shorelines of Long Island and Connecticut. Long Island artist William Sidney Mount described how local mariners in Stony Brook tried to clear ice clogging the harbor to get out in an attempt to rescue survivors.[110] One witness whose name was not recorded wrote: "The boat was seen on fire, drifting past Stony Brook, about midway of the sound, the blaze shooting up from her in columns, lighting up the waters for miles around.…Her blaze…showed her solitary and sable chimneys, standing as monuments over some mighty moving catacomb of death."[111]

While some fishermen intent on saving those on board were able to get out of their harbors in smaller boats despite the accumulated ice, the forward momentum of the steamboat before the pressure dropped in the boilers combined with the wind and tide carried the vessel away from these would-be rescuers. "An effort was made by four brave men of Southport, Connecticut, who started out in yawl boats to go to the relief of those on the burning steamer, but after a fruitless search they returned about one o'clock in the morning, almost frozen from the cold and drenched with the spray of the waves which dashed over them."[112] Captain William Tirrell of the sloop *Improvement* of Brookhaven already was out on the Sound and saw the fire. But he failed to offer assistance, reportedly claiming that the lifeboats on the *Lexington* would provide refuge and that he could not afford to lose the incoming tide to get into Setauket. He was widely denounced and almost had his captain's papers revoked. But a later investigation determined that he was twelve miles away with a contrary wind so that it was unlikely he could have saved anyone.

The most important Good Samaritan was based in Southport. Captain Oliver Meeker of the sloop *Merchant* tried to sail away from the pier, but with the tide falling, his vessel ran aground. But Meeker refused to give up, and three of the four survivors owed their lives to his persistence.

THE SURVIVORS' STORIES

Chester Hillard

Once merchant ship captain Chester Hillard decided to leave the flaming *Lexington*, he teamed up with fireman Benjamin Cox to execute his escape plan of using a cotton bale as a raft. He testified at the inquest that

> aided by one of the firemen, I put the bale up on the rail, round which we took a turn [with the rope he had cut], slipped the bale down below the [paddlewheel] guard.…We got on to the bale before we lowered it. The boat then lay broad side to the wind and we were under the lee of the

> *boat, on the larboard* [port or left] *side. We placed ourselves one on each end of the bale, facing each other. With our weight on the bale it remained about one third out of the water. The wind was pretty fresh, and we drifted at the rate of about a knot and a half* [about 1.7 miles per hour]. *We did not lash ourselves to the bale, but coiled the rope up and laid it on the bale. My companion did not like the idea of leaving the boat immediately, but wished to hold on to the* [paddlewheel] *guards. I determined to get out of the way, believing that to remain there much longer it would become pretty hot quarters. We accordingly shoved the bale round the stern.*

As Hillard picked up a board to use as a paddle or rudder to keep the narrow side of the bale facing the waves, the pair drifted away from the steamboat on their cotton raft at a rate that Hillard estimated to be almost two miles an hour. "This was just 8 o'clock by my watch, which I took out and looked at it."[113]

"At the time we left the boat there were but few persons remaining on board," Hillard recounted. Passing the ladies' cabin by the stern, which was fully ablaze, he noticed one woman in particular because her child had apparently already gone overboard and was floating about thirty feet behind the steamboat. Hillard believed she was Mrs. Russell Jarvis, who was traveling with two daughters.

> *We passed by the child so near that I could put my hand on it as it lay on its back. The lady saw us approaching the child and cried out for us to save it. I should think the child was a female from its dress. I think it had on a bonnet. The child was dead when we passed it.... We then drifted away from the boat, and in 10 minutes more we could see no persons on board except those on the forecastle. It was at the time pretty rough, and I had as much as I could do to manage my bale of cotton.*[114]

Hillard and Cox had escaped from the burning vessel, but their survival was hardly guaranteed.

> *We were sitting astride of the bale with our feet in the water; I was wet up to my middle from the water which at times washed over the bale; we were in sight of the boat all the time, till she went down, when we were about a mile distant; when we left the wreck it was cloudy, but about nine o'clock it cleared off, and we had a fine night of it until the moon went down; I looked at my watch as often as every half hour, through the night,*

Captain Hillard and his companion on the bale of cotton.

Captain Chester Hillard was the only passenger to survive. This illustration shows him sharing a cotton bale with fireman Benjamin Cox, who died from exposure. *From Warren Lazell's* Steamboat Disasters and Railroad Accidents in the United States to Which Are Appended Accounts of Recent Shipwrecks, Fires at Sea, Thrilling Incidents, etc. *published in 1846.*

the boat went down at three o'clock; it was so cold as to make it necessary for me to exert myself to keep warm, which I did by whipping my hands and arms around my body; about 4 o'clock the bale capsized with us; a heavy sea came and carried the bale over end-ways.... We managed to get to the bale on its opposite side; we at this time lost our piece of board, afterwards the bale was ungovernable and went as it liked; my companion had complained a good deal of the cold from our first setting out; he didn't seem to have that spirit about him that he ought to have had; he was continually fretting himself about things which he had no business to. He said his name was Cox, and that his wife lived in this city, at No. 11 Cherry street. He appeared to have given up all hope of our being saved. On our first starting from the boat, I gave him my vest as he had on his chest only a flannel shirt. He had on pantaloons, boots and cap.

The fireman remained on the bale after he and Hillard were thrown into the water for more than two hours, until almost daylight.

For the last half hour that he remained on the bale, he had been speechless, and seemed to have lost all use of his hands as he did not try to hold on. I rubbed him and beat his flesh, and used otherwise every effort I could to keep his blood in circulation. It was still very rough, and I was obliged to exert myself to hold on. The bale coming broad side to the sea it gave a lurch and Cox slipped off and I saw him no more. He went down without a struggle. I then got more into the middle of the bale, to make it ride as it should, and in that way continued until at least for about an hour. I got my feet on the bale and so remained until the sloop picked me up. The sea had by this time become quite smooth.

The sloop that picked up Hillard about 11:00 a.m. was the *Merchant*, which Captain Meeker had finally gotten away from the dock in Southport and through the ice to reach the Sound. "On seeing the sloop I waved my hat, to attract the attention of those on board; I was not frozen in any part," Hillard said.

He conveyed his gratitude for Meeker's efforts to the inquest jury:

> *I think Capt. M. and those on board the sloop are entitled to a great deal of credit, as they did more on the occasion than any one else. It appears that they tried during the night to get out to the aid of those on board the* Lexington, *but in coming out the sloop grounded on the bar, and they were compelled before they could get her off to lighten her of part of her cargo.… On going on board of the sloop, I had every possible attention paid me; they took me into the cabin and then cruised in search of others.*
>
> > *They picked up two other living men and the bodies of two others. The living men were Captain Manchester, pilot of the* Lexington, *and the other Charles Smith, a hand on board. One of the persons was picked up on a bale of cotton, and the other on the wheel-house.… They were both picked up within half an hour. When they were brought on board, Captain Manchester was pretty much exhausted; Smith seemed better. They put them both in bed.*[115]

Hillard said that Captain Meeker continued to search for about three hours after finding the two other survivors. But the *Merchant* located only two bodies in that time. "One of them was on a piece of the wheel-house, and the other on a piece of the wreckage," he said. "When we were about half way from the wreck to Southport, the steamboat *Nimrod* overtook us, and I went on board of her. She was bound into Bridgeport. We arrived there in about three quarters of an hour. I went ashore and went to the house of Captain Davis, an acquaintance of mine with whom I had formerly sailed— staid there that night— the next morning at 8 o'clock went on board the steamboat *Nimrod* and came to New York."[116]

Stephen Manchester

After Hillard and those with him amidships abandoned the *Lexington*, about thirty others remained on the bow with pilot Stephen Manchester. After consuming the center of the ship, the fire died down. But Manchester became convinced near midnight that the steamboat could not stay afloat much longer and decided it was time to take his chances on the water. About two hours later, by his estimation, the hulk sank in the middle of the Sound in more than one hundred feet of water northwest of Port Jefferson.

Once he decided to go over the side, Manchester told the inquest jury,

> *I then took a piece of spun yarn and made it fast to my coat, and also to the rail, and so eased myself down upon the raft. There were two or three others on it already and my weight sank it. I held onto the rope until it came up again—and when it did, I sprang up and caught a piece of railing which was in the water, and from thence got on a bale of cotton where there was a man sitting: found the bale was made fast to the railing: I took out my knife and cut it off. About the time I cut this rope off, I saw another person standing on the piece of railing—asked me if there was room for another; I made no answer, and he jumped and knocked off the man that was with me; and I hauled him on again. I caught a piece of board which was floating past me and shoved the bale clean off from the raft; and used the board to endeavor to get in shore at Crane Neck Point* [west of Port Jefferson], *but I could not succeed; but I used the board as long as I could, for exercise. When I left the wreck, I looked at my watch and it was just twelve o'clock. I think the man who was on the bale with me said his name was McKenny, and lived at New York; he died about 3 o'clock.* [It was Patrick McKenna, who the pilot later learned was a clerk at the firm of Donnelly and Hyatt.] *When I hauled him on the bale I encouraged him and told him to thrash his hands, which he did for a spell, but soon gave up pretty much. When he died he fell back on the bale and the first wave that came pushed him off it: my hands were then so frozen that I*

Captain Manchester and M'Kenna on the bale of cotton.

The pilot of the *Lexington*, Captain Stephen Manchester, survived by climbing aboard a cotton bale with the passenger who died of exposure. *From Warren Lazell's* Steamboat Disasters and Railroad Accidents in the United States to Which Are Appended Accounts of Recent Shipwrecks, Fires at Sea, Thrilling Incidents, etc. *published in 1846.*

could not use them at all; while I was on the cotton I looked at my watch; two o'clock and three miles from the wreck when she sank; the last thing I recollect was seeing the sloop, and I raised my handkerchief between my fingers, hoping they would see me; I believe they did. I was then sitting on the cotton, with my feet in the water. The cotton never rolled at all, although there were some heavy seas; the man who was on the bale [McKenna] *spoke of his wife and children, that he had kissed them the morning he left home, that he was never before through the Sound, and said he feared he would die of the cold.*

After being rescued about 11:00 a.m., Manchester said, "I was brought to Southport, where I received every possible attention."[117] An 1891 magazine account by an eyewitness stated that "Captain Manchester, whose limbs were badly frozen, was taken into the hospitable home of the Hon. Jonathan Godfrey, and after six weeks of great suffering recovered and left for home" in Providence.[118]

Charles Buckingham Smith

After the lifeboat with the captain was swamped and lost, Fireman Charles Smith testified at the inquest that

I got over the stern with the intention of getting on to the rudder; I hung by the netting, kicked in three cabin windows, and lowered myself down and got on the rudder. I had stood there but a minute or two, when several others came on there also; did not know the names of any of them, knew one of them to be a waiter. There was a boy got over the stern and I told him to drop overboard and get on a bale of cotton: he said he could not swim. I then told him to tell some of them on deck to throw over a bale of cotton. Some of them hove a bale over, which I jumped on after, and gave the boy my place. I swam to it, and got on it. I was on it until about 1:30 o'clock.

At that time I drifted back to the steamboat and got on her. There were then 10 or 12 persons hanging to different parts of the boat. [The chief engineer] *Mr. Hempstead was one of them, and one of the firemen by the name of Baum—Job Sands, a waiter—Harry Reed, the man that first woke me, and a small English boy—another coal heaver, his name was William—there was a deckhand by the name of Charles.... The rest were, as I suppose, passengers and some waiters—there were no ladies. I stayed there until 3 o'clock, when she sank. I stayed about midships, near where the fire originated.…After she began to fill, the rest jumped off.*

After she sunk, I swam to a piece of the [paddle] *guard and with four others got on it, who all perished before day-light. One of them was Harry Reed, and another, George, the fireman—the other was the boy I had given my place on the rudder—the other I don't know; I think they all perished with the cold. I shook them around and tried to exercise and rub them.*

I remained on the piece of [paddle] *guard until 2 o'clock in the afternoon, when I was taken off by the sloop* Merchant, *Captain Meeker, and was taken into Southport, where I had the best care taken of me possible. I was in my senses all the time. I swung my cap to the sloop, but they had seen me before. My feet were barely frozen, and my fingers touched a little with the frost.*[119]

He was revived and cared for at the home of a Mrs. Jelliff until able to return home to Providence.[120]

David Crowley

By far the most remarkable survival tale was that of Second Mate David Crowley. Because he was alone on his cotton bale, it never capsized and he was able to burrow into it to stay relatively warm. It was not until 9:00 p.m. on Wednesday that he drifted up along ice built up on the Long Island shore at Baiting Hollow near Riverhead—nearly fifty miles from where he had abandoned the *Lexington* two nights earlier.

Since Crowley, who had been working on vessels since 1832, could not testify at the inquest because he was recuperating at Baiting Hollow, an article was entered into the record from the *Corrector* of Sag Harbor, the most prominent weekly newspaper on Long Island at the time. (There were no daily newspapers east of Brooklyn.) The newspaper story was based on an interview with a Mr. Southgate, who had returned to Sag Harbor after having talked to Crowley in Baiting Hollow.[121]

According to the *Corrector*, after Crowley discovered the boat was on fire, "he soon took to a plank, but shortly left it for a bale of cotton, on which he drifted until Wednesday evening, when he landed at New Gulley, opposite River Head [Riverhead], and made his way to the house of Matthias Hutchinson; having drifted in that time somewhere about 50 miles, and absolutely *sleeping* at times." While he was drifting east on the Sound, "he often saw the blaze [from the *Lexington*] shooting up from her in columns, lighting the whole Sound, and then dying away in darkness."[122]

Crowley almost was rescued the day after the fire.

> *On Tuesday, the morning after the misfortune, he saw the sloop* Merchant *pick up one or two persons; he endeavored, by holding up his waistcoat, to attract their notice, but without success. When the night of that day came on, he thought himself near Falkland* [Falkner] *Island* [three miles south of Guilford, Connecticut, and east of New Haven], *and expected to drift ashore there, but, finding himself exhausted, he, miraculous to state, composed himself on his bale of cotton, went to sleep, and slept soundly until morning! Much revived by his sleep, he continued, through the following day, to make every exertion, his situation permitted, to reach the land* [Long Island], *which however, he did not do until night. When landed, he scaled the high bank* [of ice] *on the shore, when a light at a distance attracted his notice; he followed its direction until he reached the hospitable mansion of Mr. Huntington* [Hutchinson] *at the moment his son had just arrived there, and was relating the particulars of the loss of the* Lexington. [The family did not know about the fate of the *Lexington* until told about it by Crowley as he began to recover.] *His unexpected appearance, pale and wretched, with his waistcoat around his head, naturally created sensations of pity and astonishment. He received all the care and attention his helpless and miserable situation required.*[123]

The *Long Island Democrat* marveled that Crowley had "been 40 hours exposed to the severity of the weather." When his cotton bale ran aground on the ice along the shore, Crowley, fearful of falling through the ice after all he had endured, crawled to the beach. He stumbled nearly a mile to the house of Matthias and Mary Hutchinson and knocked on the door with the last of his strength before passing out.

Mary Hutchinson described the scene in a book of essays written by her grandson W.J. Hutchinson in 1887:

> *The winter's night of Wednesday, January 15, 1840, was one of intense cold. I was sitting up much later than usual: the occasion of it being one of the periodical and brief visits which my eldest son, a merchant of New York, was in the habit of making to his early home. We had spent the evening in conversation, and were just about to close it with family devotions, when there was a feeble knock at the kitchen door, followed by a*

faint cry of distress. On opening the door we discovered the prostate figure of a young man about twenty-five years of age and of sturdy proportions, and without coat or hat. We instantly carried him into the house in an insensible condition, and then saw that his hands and arms resembled marble. They were solidly frozen, as his feet also proved to be once we had cut off his boots. We immediately removed him to a cold room, and immersed his extremities in cold water. During the night we cautiously raised the temperature of the water, and before morning the poor fellow had revived sufficiently to drink a few spoonfuls of beef tea, and to articulate a few words. He then made known to us the startling intelligence, that a popular steamboat plying between New York and Stonington had been burned to the water's edge; and that of a company of one hundred souls he was probably the only survivor.... The first request that Mr. Crowley made the next day was that the bale of cotton might be secured, as a souvenir of the imminent perils for which he had passed. This was done.[124]

Mary Hutchinson said that "it seems incredible that a human being could endure such a degree of cold through such an extent of time. It is not probable that a parallel case can be found, especially when it is remembered that during his drift he had not a particle of nourishment."[125]

A doctor summoned by the Hutchinsons expected Crowley would lose his toes and a finger. One report said he ultimately lost two toes on each foot. But W.J. Hutchinson wrote that "at the end of nine months Mr. Crowley left my grandmother's house, restored to health, and without a single trace remaining of his frostbites."[126]

Hutchinson ended his chapter published in 1887 by noting that

Mr. Crowley is yet serving the same steamboat line in whose employment he was when he met with his great adventure. He is now seventy-two years old, but wears his years so lightly that one would suppose him to be twenty years younger. Every night he passes the spot where the Lexington *burned. May he enjoy the life for which he made so gallant a fight against fire, water, cold, and hunger.*[127]

When Crowley was finally healthy enough to return home to Providence after nine months, he took his cotton bale with him. Newspaper accounts had him displaying it in his living room, although Hutchinson wrote that he stored it out of sight at the request of his mother, who did not want to be reminded of his ordeal. In any case, Crowley kept the bale until late in the Civil War, when the price of cotton, produced in the belligerent Confederate states and not in the North, rose to $1.50 per pound (more than $27.00 today) and he sold it, reportedly to be made into uniforms for Union soldiers. The *New York Times* reprinted an item from the *Providence Journal* on June 20, 1864, about Crowley's cotton bale. The short article concluded by saying: "This bale of cotton Mr. CROWLEY has preserved with religious care until the present time, but the price of the staple to-day has brought out the sacred relic for sale. It is of remarkable quality, and the three hundred pound bale is worth from four to five hundred dollars," or more than $9,000 today.[128] Supposedly, Crowley's cotton was the basis for a Lexington brand of textiles. Cotton from some of the other recovered bales was made into souvenir shirts.

Three crew members and one passenger survived the fire and sinking while up to 146 passengers and crew died in the first—and worst ever—steamboat fire on Long Island Sound. And the hulk of the *Lexington* lay on the bottom in more than one hundred feet of water northwest of Port Jefferson and west of today's Stratford Shoal Middle Ground Lighthouse.

5

REACTION AND RECOVERY

The first fatal steamboat accident on Long Island Sound produced harrowing stories of people drowning in icy waters or being burned to death as well as gripping tales of survival. So it's not surprising that the loss of the *Lexington* generated a huge amount of newspaper coverage in 1840.

Cynthia Kierner wrote in *Inventing Disaster* that

> *for several reasons, the wreck of the* Lexington—*one of the largest, fastest, and most luxurious ships that sailed on the Long Island Sound— was a bigger story than most.... The* Lexington *featured some famous and well-connected characters.... Equally significant, the* Lexington *story played out in public over several months, as local newspapers and benevolent citizens sought aid for victims' families, as more bodies washed ashore, and as survivors and experts rehashed the gruesome episode in a well-publicized eight-day coroner's inquest.*[129]

Newspapers in Bridgeport, Connecticut, situated near where the drama played out and near where three of the survivors were taken, apparently were the first to report on the fire. On Tuesday evening, January 11, one day after the disaster, the *Republican Standard* ran this bold headline: "APPALLING CALAMITY. STEAMBOAT LEXINGTON DESTROYED BY FIRE, AND NEARLY TWO HUNDRED LIVES LOST." The long story was based on interviewing survivor Chester Hillard (spelled Hilliard, as was often the case early on). After describing his rescue, the paper reported that the pilot and a fireman had also been rescued by the *Merchant*. "Both were nearly insensible. It is surprising that any should have survived the exposure….The account which we have given of this awful catastrophe, is exceedingly imperfect. It may be well imagined that our informant is hardly in a situation to furnish many details."

The newspaper also quoted an extra edition of another unnamed Bridgeport newspaper:

> *Our citizens were alarmed on Monday evening by the appearance of a great light at some distance west, on the Sound, which was generally believed to be a steamboat on fire. Nothing conclusive, however was heard, in regard to it till the arrival of our boat* [presumably a regularly scheduled steamboat] *from New York on Tuesday afternoon, which brought the melancholy intelligence that the light, was occasioned by the conflagration of the Steamboat* Lexington, *which was entirely destroyed, and that all on board except three perished.…The deaths of the sufferers were awful—fire water! frost and cold! Oh God! Oh God! can human imagination picture a death more horrible?*

The newspaper added that the "*Lexington* had $60,000 in specie [coins] on board; $16,000 of this was owned by the Merchants' bank of Boston. She was insured against fire."

With the slower communication channels of the time, the early information was spotty and inaccurate. And unlike newspapers of today, there was little attempt to separate reporting the news from offering opinion.

> *We are told that this boat had been condemned, some months since, as unseaworthy, but the company insisted on running her.*
>
> *When she came on last Friday, she took fire, and the passengers never expected to reach New York alive; and yet she was sent on another trip, crowded with freight and passengers, unseaworthy, with tiller ropes, and unskilful men, and she had been destroyed by fire, with 100 precious lives.*
>
> *We think that the Directors of this Company ought to be indicted by the Grand Jury, for putting their worst boat on the line during the worst weather, and overloading her with freight.…We never saw public indignation so much aroused, and all the Directors are deeply censured.…The* Lexington *has been fined for not having wires to her tillers* [not true, according to the testimony at the inquest], *and yet she evaded the law again. Over thirty stores were shut in the city as soon as the news was received.*

The Bridgeport newspaper added this improbable detail: "Captain HILLARD was saved from perishing by frost, because his body was in the water, and his head only out. He is now at the United States Hotel."

The account, which noted that the *Lexington* drifted with the tide until it sank at 3:00 a.m. off Bridgeport Harbor, continued:

> *It is feared that Professor LONGFELLOW* [poet Henry Wadsworth Longfellow], *is lost in her; the most correct list was burnt up on board the boat; perhaps no one will ever know all that were lost in her. The thought is awful. FINN, the comedian, the wit, the humorist, died this awful death. The German Professor in Harvard University, was there. Captains KIMBALL and FOSTER, had just arrived from South America, and were going on a visit to their friends. Two brothers named WINSLOW, (with their sister and mother) were taking, to Boston, the corpse of their brother, who died here a few days since....It is possible that some one or two others may be saved, but it is hardly probable. The thought is heart-rending.*

As it turned out, the victims of the *Lexington* disaster did not include Henry Wadsworth Longfellow. Several authors, including Clive Cussler, have written that Longfellow was in New York to discuss with editor Park Benjamin editorial changes to his poem *The Wreck of the Hesperus*, which was to be published in the *New York World*. Supposedly, Longfellow had tickets to sail on the *Lexington* but was delayed because the meeting ran long and missed the departure. However, at least five biographies of the poet do not even mention the *Lexington*, which would be surprising if he narrowly escaped death. More importantly, the poet writes about the *Lexington* in a letter to his

Poet Henry Wadsworth Longfellow was initially reported to have been aboard the *Lexington* but was not. *Library of Congress.*

father, Stephen, from his home in Cambridge on January 16, three days after the disaster, with no mention of any plans to have been on board. Longfellow wrote:

> *What a horrid accident the burning of the* Lexington *was! You will see the accounts in the papers. But I fear the whole truth will not be told.*

The boat was not sea-worthy. One fortnight ago Mr. Dana (a friend of mine) went to New York in the same boat. He writes, that she took fire then also, but fortunately there was no cotton on board. The engine seemed much out of order then, and stopped six times during the night. Taking a deck-load of cotton, with 150 passengers, was intolerable. I have not heard any particulars, save that Dr. [Charles] Follen and wife were on board. Only three saved.

He added at the end of the letter that "*Mrs.* Follen was *not* on board the *Lexington; the Dr.* was. He seemed to *fear* this boat, having been in her before, and had resolved never to go in her again; but was obliged to, on account of urgent necessity of his return. He said to one of his friends: 'if anything happens to the *Lexn.* you need not be alarmed on my account, as I shall never go in her again.'" In a previous letter dated January 10 from Cambridge, Longfellow wrote to his father that he had just returned home that evening from Hartford, Connecticut, after three weeks in New York City giving lectures: "I hoped to have been with you before this time; but have been delayed by the bad weather, and detained in New York longer than I anticipated.…My lectures went off very well; though I was quite ill with an influenza all the time." He writes that he had planned to come home by steamboat but

on Saturday night the Sound being frozen as far as Hurl-gate [Hell Gate], *so as to prevent any steamer's going, I started in the mail-stage, in a drizzling, foggy rain, the roads very bad and everything afloat… and about one o'clock the driver went off the road, and pitched us into a ditch four feet deep. There were three* inside *besides myself; and a dozen mail-bags. I was alone on the front seat, and in the upset, nothing came upon me but these bags. Only one passenger was hurt.….On a post-mortem examination of the carriage I found a pile of stones within a foot of where my head came down. Had there not been snow in the ditch I should have been severely hurt.*

So the real story is Longfellow narrowly escaped serious injury or death on his return to Boston, but it had nothing to do with the steamboat. He also makes no mention of meeting with his editor to go over the new poem. But the most important fact is that he was home in Massachusetts three days before the final voyage of the *Lexington*, so it is clear he had no connection to the vessel's fatal voyage other than apparently knowing

DREADFUL DISASTER!

DAILY HERALD (NEW HAVEN) EXTRA, MONDAY EVENING, JANUARY 14.

THE STEAMBOAT LEXINGTON BURNT, AND NEARLY TWO HUNDRED OF THE PASSENGERS AND CREW DESTROYED.

OFFICE OF THE REPUBLICAN STANDARD, *Bridgeport, Tuesday Evening, Jan. 14.*

APPALLING CALAMITY !—*Steamboat Lexington destroyed by fire, and nearly two hundred lives lost !* The Lexington left New York for Stonington on Monday, at 3 o'clock P. M. having, it is believed, about ONE HUNDRED AND FIFTY PASSENGERS. A large quantity of cotton was placed upon her decks. At 7 o'clock, when about two miles from Eaton's Neck, the cotton took fire near the smoke-pipe.

The initial report of the disaster in the *Long Island Star*, a Brooklyn daily newspaper.

Charles Follen, who likely would have been in his circle of friends and acquaintances in Boston.[130]

Others did avoid a likely demise. A Dr. Weeks of New York City had boarded the *Lexington* when he received a letter alerting him that his mother had died. He had his luggage removed and left the vessel before it sailed. Another lucky passenger identified only as C. Woodward, a tobacconist from Philadelphia, made it aboard only to realize he had forgotten something. When he went to retrieve it, he returned too late to make the departure, according to the *Commercial Advertiser and Journal* issue of January 21.

The New York City dailies began reporting on the sinking the day after the Bridgeport newspapers. As they described the "appalling calamity," one letter writer noted that "the city was thrown into an awful state of consternation and alarm."[131]

From New York, Kierner traced the spread of the news slowly across the rest of the country. The original Bridgeport *Republican Standard* report appeared on January 22 in the *Ohio State Journal* and three days later the news ran in the *Kalamazoo Gazette* in Michigan. It took until the end of the month to reach New Orleans, where the *Daily Picayune* wrote of "the shrieks, the screams of human beings being hunted by one element to perish in another—driven by fire into the sea in night, and in the depths of winter. Mothers with their babies, fathers, brothers, expired in the waves, giving their last cries to the un-pitying wind."

As the story unfolded, well-meaning citizens organized to help the families of the victims. In New York, a group of "philanthropic young men" visited widows of workers who had died in the disaster and, after learning that they were destitute, began to raise money to be distributed by the Female Assistance Society, a local charity. Others donated money as rewards for the recovery of bodies of victims whose families were too poor to do so.[132] There were also benefit concerts.

THE RECOVERY EFFORTS

Only sixteen bodies would be found.

Captain Meeker's sloop *Merchant* recovered two bodies. The other fourteen were picked up by other vessels or washed up on beaches. The frigid water carried the rest to the bottom of the Sound.

The Transportation Company dispatched Captain Joseph J. Comstock to search for bodies and recover any luggage and company property he could find. The steamboat *Statesman* under the command of Captain George Peck was chartered for the operation. But it did not depart until Thursday.

Determining where to look was a problem because witnesses observed the burning ship from Eatons Neck north of Huntington out east to Crane's Neck west of Port Jefferson. The keeper of the Old Field Point Lighthouse at Crane's Neck said he saw the flames disappear about three o'clock in the morning about four miles to the north and slightly west, which seemed like the most reliable report. (The wreck was ultimately located by author Clive Cussler in 1983 to the east of the position cited by the lighthouse keeper, which makes sense because the wind and current carried the hulk northeastward after the fire burned out before it sank.) After two days, only five additional bodies beyond the two found by Meeker on the *Merchant* were recovered by Comstock.[133]

While his recovery crew had a difficult time finding victims, their possessions, debris and eight more bodies washed up along miles of Long Island and Connecticut coastline. The remnants of the wreck found included the ship's two-foot-long nameplate from the side of the wheelhouse, a swamped lifeboat and luggage. With the temperature stuck at four degrees below zero hampering the recovery effort, Comstock called off his operation as hopeless, even though the search had a particular importance for him: his brother, Jesse, had sailed as clerk of the *Lexington*. His body was never found.[134] On January 16, Comstock placed an ad in the Bridgeport *Republican Standard* that read:

> *A reward of $100 will be paid for the recovery of the body of Mr. Jesse Comstock, late clerk of the steamboat, "Lexington," and giving information of the same in any New York paper. He was aged 20 years, almost five feet, two or three inches in height, rather thick-set, light complexion and light hair, with a high forehead. His dress consisted of a black frock coat, dark-mixed pantaloons and figured woolen vest; a cotton shirt, marked J.C., or name in full, and knit lamb's wool, do. [ditto], cotton drawers and cotton stockings. He had on his person a small gold watch and short gold chain.[135]*

Many similar advertisements ran in papers around the region.

The *New York Journal of Commerce* reported on January 18, five days after the fire, on the trip by the *Statesman* and added that "the Postmaster at Southport [Connecticut] writes that the bodies of Mr. [Cortland] Hempstead, of Brooklyn, first Engineer, and that of Job Sands, head waiter, had been picked up and taken into that place."

And then it added a postscript: Francis Dow, brother of Mr. R.W. Dow, one of the passengers, had arrived the previous evening from Brookhaven, Long Island:

> *From him we learn that five bodies had been found when he left…that of Philo Upson of Egremont, Mass. Which drifted ashore at Old Field Point; those of two seamen, which went ashore at Miller's Place [today's Miller Place]; that of a child; and that of a young man, supposed to be either Mr. Dow or Mr. Waterbury, of this city. His face being covered thickly with ice, which it was thought in-expedient to remove until brought to the city, it was difficult to identify him with certainty.*

Dow also told the newspaper that

> *at one time the burning steamboat was within a mile and a half of the L.I. shore; but probably from the tiller chains giving way, she soon rapidly*

receded. A boat put out from the shore at one time, and rowed two or three miles, but finding the Lexington *was increasing her distance, returned. It was low tide, and none of the sloops and schooners could be got out. Some of the inhabitants say they heard two explosions in the night, which they now suppose to have been caused by the bursting of the boilers.*

Also on January 18, the *New York Evening Tattler* published a special "extra" edition to print a letter it had received from Captain Comstock about his search for bodies. That letter may have been the source for the often-repeated story about the sloop *Improvement* not coming to the rescue.

Steamboat Statesman
Friday Night, Jan. 17th, 1840
To the editor of the Evening Tattler—

Gentleman—We are now returning to New York, having searched the shore of Long Island from Huntington to Fresh Pond landing, a distance, taking into account consideration the depth of the bays and inlets, of nearly 90 miles, every rod [a rod is 16.5 feet] *of which I think has been thoroughly examined by those on board the boat with me, and others on shore who came down by land. We have been enabled to regain, however, only five bodies.*

One is identified as being that of Mr. Stephen Waterbury, of the firm of Mead & Waterbury, of New York—On another was found a memorandum book, with the name of Philo Upson of South Egremont, Mass., one a little boy probably three or four years old.

From the appearance of the others, they are probably deck hands of the boat.

We have 30 packages of baggage and the life boat of the Lexington. *These with the bodies, we are now conveying to New York.*

From Crane's Neck light [Old Field Point Lighthouse] *to Old Man's landing* [today's Mount Sinai] *12 or 15 miles East including the deep bays adjacent, is covered with pieces of the wreck, among which I noticed her name upon the siding* [the vessel's nameplate from the side of the wheelhouse], *nearly in full length, large pieces of her* [paddle] *guards, and portions of almost every part of the boat—all of which is mostly burnt to a coal. We found one of her quarter* [life] *boats from which three of the bodies now in our possession were taken; she is very slightly damaged.*

The boat [the *Statesman*] *is at a place called Miller's Landing* [probably today's Miller Place], *and here we learned that a man*

[Second Mate David Crowley] *came ashore on a bale of cotton alive, 15 miles to the eastward of this place, to which I immediately repaired. Here I could effect no landing owing to the large quantities of ice drifted in by the stormy northerly wind. We however, crowded in near enough to the shore to converse with persons drawn to the beach by our signals, and from them learned the fact that Mr. David Crawley* [Crowley], *second mate of the* Lexington, *had drifted ashore upon a bale of cotton on Wednesday night at 9 o'clock, after being 48 hours exposed to the severity of the weather—after which he made his way through large quantities of ice, and swam before gaining the beach, and then walked three quarters of a mile to a house—his hands are little frozen—his feet and legs considerably so—he is not able, however, to be moved for the present—this I have been told by a person who saw him today—it appears…the weather and ice has completely blocked up the shores. The northerly winds kept driving the ice to leeward, and every thing not floating very light would naturally be buried beneath this constant accumulation of ice. In consequence of this, I think we have been prevented from procuring many bodies that, in more moderate weather, could have been seen.*

Capt. Wm Terrel, master of the sloop Improvement, *was with his vessel within 4 or 5 miles of the* Lexington *at the time she commenced burning, and thinks if he had immediately repaired to her assistance, he would have been able to have saved a great number of lives. The reason he gives for not doing so is that he would have lost his tide over the Bar to the Port to which he was bound, and accordingly pursued his demon-like course, leaving upwards of 100 persons to die the worst of deaths.*

Respectfully yours
Joseph J. Comstock

It was not an exaggeration when the *Long-Island Star*, printed in Brooklyn, on Monday evening, January 20, wrote that "the awful calamity and great loss of life by the burning of the *Lexington*, continues to engross the public mind." Under a headline of "Steam Boat *Lexington*, Further Particulars of the Disaster," the newspaper asked on page 2:

Who has not lost a friend? So many persons were involved in that overwhelming affliction, that the whole community appear to feel it, and deeply to sympathize with the immediate relatives of the sufferers. There is some consolation in believing that the loss of life was not so great as that first apprehended. It is now stated at not far from one hundred, including both passengers and crew. [The actual number was up to 146.] *The list of persons supposed to be lost…is now ascertained to be defective in many particulars.*

But even though accurate information was hard to come by, the newspaper had additional names to add "to the list of sufferers" reprinted from the *New York Express*. These include several seafarers, including a Captain "Childs," supposedly the brother of George Child, captain of the *Lexington*, although that name does not appear on the final list of passengers and crew. It also named a Captain Mattison, who is on the final list with no first name given. A "Mr. McFarland of Portland, mate on the barque *Brontes*," turned out to be David MacFarlane, mate of the brig *Clarion*. It also listed "seamen John Walker and Isaac Howes, residents of Cambridgeport [a neighborhood in Cambridge, Massachusetts], who had recently sailed on the brig *Raymond* out of New Orleans," but they do not appear on the final list. Robert Blake, president of the Bank of Wrentham in Wrentham, Massachusetts, was initially and erroneously reported to have survived by clinging to a cotton bale for five days before being picked up by an outbound vessel and returned to his home. William H. Wilson, a grocer from Williamsburg in Brooklyn, and "Elias Brown Jr. of Providence, 'lately married to a Miss Avery of Stonington,'" were also initially reported to have survived.

The *Star* noted that

Mr. Finn, the comedian, was returning to his home at Newport, where a wife and nine [he had twelve] *children deplore his premature death. He owned a handsome farm and villa at that place.….Mr. Phelps, among the victims, was a gentleman of great enterprise, well-known and highly esteemed in our city. He acquired a large fortune in a contract for paving at New Orleans, some years since, and owned a beautiful mansion at Stonington, celebrated for its taste and arrangement, but now a house of mourning by this sad event, which has bereaved his family for their head.*

The *Star* provided some background for its readers and advice to the steamboat companies:

In warm weather, steamboats on the Sound are provided with a great number of buckets standing full of water ready at a moment's notice to extinguish any fire. In cold weather, it is impossible to have buckets filled with water, nor can a person dip a bucket of water, from the side when the boat is going twelve miles an hour. To be always provided, a rotary pump should be placed forward and also aft—the pipe running through the cabin, would prevent it from freezing. In this way it would always be ready for any emergency.[136]

On January 21, the *Providence Journal* reprinted a letter written to the mother of Second Mate David Crowley penned by Samuel Hutchinson, son of the couple who had taken in Crowley, and mailed from Riverhead five days earlier.

Madam—Your son who was on board the Steam Boat Lexington, *wishes me to inform you of the loss of the boat by fire, on Monday evening last, he was floated about the Sound for two days and nights, on a bale of Cotton, and came ashore at this place last evening, he, was without a coat or hat, and was very much exhausted and his feet and hands much frozen; we have taken the best of care of him we could by soaking his feet and hands in water to take the frost out, but they are still very sore, he is at the house of Matthias Hutchinson, my father, of this township, living near the Sound Shore. I have just seen the Doctor, and sent him to see your son, and we will do the best we can. My own residence is in New York, at No. 284 Pearl street. I am now here on a visit, but expect to be in the city on Monday next where, if you wish any further information, you can address me. Your son thinks that a very large proportion of the passengers and crew of the* Lexington *were drowned.*
Very respectively, yours,
Samuel Hutchinson

There were new details on recovery of bodies in the New York *Commercial Advertiser* on January 22. It reported that the remains of Henry S. Craig, N. Brackett, William A. Green (Greene) of Providence and David Green (Greene) of Philadelphia, agent for the Minot Shoe Company, had been picked up at "River Head" (Riverhead), Long Island, the day before. They were being held by the Suffolk County coroner, who was expected to deliver them to New York on the afternoon of publication.

The newspaper also printed an update to the previous information:

Since the above was [set] in type, we have received the following from the Steamboat company: The coroner has accompanied them to Brooklyn, where they arrived, and are momently expected at the depot of the Company, pier No. 1, Battery place, New York.

Information has been sent from the office of the Company to the friends of these gentlemen....The bodies are in boxes with the names on them. It is said that $15,000 was found on the body of Mr. Wm. A. Green [Greene] and is in the hands of the Coroner. The bodies were in one of the quarter boats of the Lexington, *which was found frozen in at Stonybrook [Stony Brook] harbor.*

The newspaper's update included information about cargo recovered:

Information has also reached the office that [wreckmaster] *Captain Woolsey has found a writing desk belonging to Capt. Eleazer Kimbail, [Kimball] with $430.*

1 trunk   marked J.C. Brown
1 do [ditto]   belonging to Mrs. [Henry A.] Winslow,
1 do   do Charles Bosworth
1 do   do William Marshall
Which Capt. Woolsay has in charge.

Charles Bosworth and William Marshall are not listed on the final passenger list.

After the initial coverage of the disaster and search for bodies, additional accounts began to surface of people who had the good fortune to miss the departure of the *Lexington* and likely death. The *Commercial Advertiser* wrote about two of these fortunate individuals in its January 22 coverage, reprinting items from the New York *Journal of Commerce*. "The following stories show on how small a circumstance our life sometimes depends," the editors noted.

When the Philadelphia morning boat arrived on Monday the 13th, one of the gentlemen passengers called a hack and agreed with the driver to take him to Eighth street. Another gentleman, being about to get in, the former admonished the driver that he must not zig zag about the city, but go directly to Eighth street. "Yes Sir" said the driver, "I will take you first; it will not be out of the way for this gentleman." When the hack had gone on some distance, the gentlemen fell into a conversation and the second one stated that he was on his way to Boston, and was going to the Providence boat; "To the Providence boat, sir?" exclaimed the other; "Why, we started from the very next pier to the Providence boat, and here this rascal of a hackman is taking you on a journey of three miles, and you will certainly be too late." Such was the fact…for the Lexington *had gone when the hack returned, and so the man's life was saved. This story shows the advantage of being cheated, and is calculated, not to make us approve of fraud, but to rejoice that there is a Providence which can bring so much good out of so vexatious an evil.*

One of our citizens who was very anxious to go to Boston in the boat on Monday evening, was, by a series of apparent untoward circumstances, prevented from finishing his business at Philadelphia in time to return here on Saturday, he remained at Philadelphia until Monday. His Boston trip was accordingly deferred and his life saved. This shows the advantage of keeping the Sabbath.

While news of the disaster filled the daily newspapers in the region starting on the day after the sinking, it was not until the following week that weekly newspapers could join in the coverage. On January 24, the *Long-Islander*, a Long Island weekly newspaper founded by poet Walt Whitman in Huntington, near where the fire was first observed, filled much of a page with news of the steamboat mishap. Under a headline that read "Loss of the *Lexington*!" the paper wrote—with tangled syntax and evident cultural snobbery—that

it is our melancholy duty to inform our readers of the most appalling accident that has occurred so near to their homes for many years. The degree of melancholy which was spread over the community by the disastrous wrecks of the Bristol *and* Mexico [ships carrying Irish immigrants that wrecked on the Atlantic Ocean coastline of Long Island within two months in the winter of 1836–37 with the loss of 215 passengers and crew] *will bear but little comparison with that which must be occasioned by the dreadful accident which has occurred in our vicinity, by which about one hundred human beings—citizens of our own country—and immediately connected with a large community by the ties of kindred and friendship, have perished. The cities of New York, Boston, Providence, as well as some sections at our own Island, will have cause to remember a long time, the disastrous occurrence which is related below. Indeed, there are a few of us who cannot refer in the melancholy list to the name of some personal acquaintance.*

The weekly then went on to reprint accounts from daily newspapers in the region, including the *Bridgeport Farmer*, which noted that the *Statesman* had recovered the bodies of Stephen Waterbury, Philo Upson and crew members Benjamin Ledoux (Laden) and Silas Thornburg (Thurber, the first mate) and a boy about five years old. "The arms and face of the child are much scorched; its face is frightfully distorted with the agonies of its dreadful death. The faces of both seamen are also shockingly scorched, particularly that of one man, whose left eye seems to have been burned out. All the bodies are frozen stiff, and partially covered with ice." The newspaper noted that David Crowley, after his two days on the cotton bale, "has doubtless been the most severe sufferer....His extremities were as stiff as marble."

The *Long-Islander* coverage included an article about efforts of relatives of the missing to find their bodies:

> The following rewards have been offered for the recovery of the bodies of the following persons, who were passengers on board the Lexington;—$100 for the body of Samuel Henry, late of Manchester, Eng. aged about 35 years, light complexion, hair black, with a little gray, 5 ft. 6 or 7 inches in height, information to be given to Pickersgill & Co., New York, or to J.N. Lloyd, Lloyd's Neck.
>
> Also Chas. W. Woolsey, of Boston, 38 years of age, 5 ft. 9 in. high, stout build, bushy whiskers, and a scar on one side of his face, information to be given to Geo. W. Woolsey, 27 Clinton Place., Wm. C. Woolsey, 21 Hanover st., N.Y. or J.N. Lloyd, Lloyds Neck.

Weeks after the demise of the *Lexington*, the story continued to be of interest to news publications beyond the region. Baltimore-based *Niles' National Register* provided extensive coverage in its issue of February 8:

> Capt. Brown, of Smithtown, who appears to be an honest, plainspoken man, relates a circumstance in connection with the discovery of these [four] bodies, which we should not relate, if he did not tell it with an apparent conviction of its truth. He says that on Monday night he dreamed that a [life]boat had come on shore in Smithtown Bay, that he in consequence rose before daylight and went to the spot, where, about half an hour after sunrise, he discovered the boat, and immediately called upon his neighbors and the coroner, Darling D. Whitney, Esq. to accompany him to secure the bodies. This was done with great care, and in a way to prevent even the suspicion that anyone of the valuable property about the bodies, have been disturbed.

Niles' National Register also stated that "the body of Mr. Finn, the comedian, one of the passengers in the *Lexington*, has been recovered. It was found floating, with a life preserver attached to it." But the body of Finn, who had written an eerily prophetic poem called "The Funeral at Sea," was never recovered. A benefit was held at the Tremont Theatre in Boston to support the actor's widow and twelve children, the *Daily Pennsylvanian* reported on February 1. *Niles'* also said that the body of John Marshall, "a glass blower who has left a wife and three children," had been recovered, but that name does not appear in the final list of victims. The newspaper reprinted an item from the *Providence Journal* that stated, "Several suits have been commenced against the company by persons in the city, who had goods on board of the *Lexington*." One of the suits, brought by the Merchants' Bank of Boston, would go all the way to the U.S. Supreme Court. (See chapter 8.)

Niles' also reprinted an account from the *New York Enquirer* of January 8 about Comstock's recovery trip on the *Statesman*. After detailing the initial stops along both shores, the paper wrote that Comstock "on arriving off Oldfield [Old Field] Point, there perceived wagons loading articles that had apparently drifted ashore. On landing, it was found that these were trunks and baggage belonging to the passengers of the *Lexington*, and the wreck master there had taken them under his charge." The article noted that the body of Philo Upson of Egremont, Massachusetts, wearing a life preserver, had washed ashore. "From the papers about him it is supposed he followed the business of a patent leather dresser." Upson was, in fact, a successful entrepreneur who owned a quarry and other businesses.

The newspaper also wrote about a letter received from the postmaster of Southport, Connecticut, that said, "The bodies of Mr. Hempstead, of Brooklyn [first engineer] and that of Job Sands [head waiter], a colored man, have floated ashore at that place."

The publication also relayed information received from the driver of the Riverhead stage, who had arrived in the city via the Long Island Rail Road with information about an unnamed survivor, who would have been Second Mate David Crowley: "He floated ashore opposite Riverhead, about forty miles beyond the place where the disaster occurred—he was unable to give his name, but strong hopes were expressed by the physicians in attendance that he would recover. He was left at the house of Mr. Terry [Hutchinson]. This later information appears to us rather apocryphal. We have endeavored to trace it to an authentic source, but without success."

The newspaper added that "this much, however, we believe is true, that one of the letter bags on board the *Lexington* has been picked up at Riverhead or Brookhaven, marked 'Charlestown' and arrived at the post office here yesterday afternoon." *Niles'* went on to say:

> Late last evening we heard that Mr. Dow, the brother of one of the unfortunate passengers [R.W. Dow of New York City], had returned in the belief that he found the corpse of him he sought, but it was so disfigured by ice and in other ways, that he cannot speak positively. All kinds of rumors were afloat as to the bodies washed ashore on Long Island. One individual was said to have reached the city with information that the person who had come ashore at Riverhead, had died on the following day, another that four more dead bodies had been found there. We merely mention these reports, repeating that after much inquiry we could trace them to no satisfactory source.

The unsubstantiated story about the callous captain of the *Improvement* was repeated:

> It will be scarcely credited, yet we have heard from two or three quarters, and one of which is entitled to every consideration, that the sloop Improvement, *of Brookhaven, was inside* [in sight] *of the burning steamboat during the whole time of the conflagration. That the hand on deck, on seeing the flames, went below and called upon the captain who was in his berth. He came on deck, said it must be a steamboat, and then turned in again. It is painful even to relate such an instance of brutal indifference to human suffering.*

Niles' reprinted in an item from the New York *Journal of Commerce* that on the morning after the fire:

> Mr. Nathaniel Brown, a worthy farmer near Stoney [Stony] Brook, Long Island, discovered one of the boats of the Lexington *firmly embedded in the ice, about half a mile from the shore. The boat was itself full of ice, but on cutting it out, the bodies of Mr.* [H.C.] Craig [of New York], *and Mr.* [Charles] Brackett, *of New York, Mr. Wm. A. Green* [Greene], *of Providence, and Mr. David Green* [Greene], *of Philadelphia, were found. On all of the bodies were found the letters and articles of value which the passengers had before the accident. In the pocket of Mr. Green, of Providence, was found $15,000 in bank bills, sundry letters, &c.* [etc.] *All of the bodies were brought to New York. It is presumed that these gentlemen were in*

the boat when it was lowered. It struck the water bow first and was capsized, and the presumption is, that being strong, they held on, and found themselves in the boat when she righted, but the boat full of water. Having no means of bailing out the water, and doubtless chilled with cold and exposure, the unhappy men were only sustained with their faces above the surface, and finally, when their strength failed, their heads fell upon the cross seats, where they were found. Mr. Green, of Providence, in the bow, and Mr. Craig, in the stern, the others in the centre. The place where the boat was found is the head of the bay, two miles from the sea, with only a very narrow inlet, and there can be but little doubt the boat floated into the position where it was found, within twenty-four hours of the disaster.

The *Brooklyn Daily Eagle* reported on the sixtieth anniversary of the disaster on January 14, 1900, that Dr. Darling Whitney, the coroner of Suffolk County, held an inquest on the bodies of William Albert Greene of Providence and Henry J. Craig of Providence, although he was actually from New York, who were found frozen in the lifeboat that came ashore in Smithtown Bay. "Upon the body of William Albert Green were found sixty-five letters addressed to persons and business firms of Providence and other places.…Upon Mr. Green's person was also found $6,550 in bank notes upon the Providence Bank of Rhode Island."[137]

Referring to the inquest held in New York after the disaster, *Niles' National Register* in its 1840 reporting also quoted the *New York Times* as saying that "the coroner, has in this case, been throughout untiring and his zeal and exertions, to produce in evidence, every fact and circumstance that could by any possibility, be brought to bear upon the matter, under investigation."

Niles' continued its coverage in its February 15 issue. It contained a story from an unnamed New York City newspaper about a public meeting held in Boston the previous week on the destruction of the *Lexington*. The session, led by the mayor, culminated with the appointment of a committee of fifteen charged with investigating the subject of steamboat disasters. Another committee of five members was appointed to raise the subject with the state legislature. "Some of the resolutions, unanimously adopted, censuring the company, and pronouncing the boat to be 'unsafe for winter navigation,' are in the face of facts, brought out here before the coroner's inquest," the newspaper stated. This was a rare case of a newspaper not joining in the widespread condemnation of the owners and crew of the *Lexington* based on the inquest jury findings, which were contradicted by much of the expert testimony.

Besides newspaper editorials and public meetings, there were many sermons lamenting the suffering of the victims, denouncing the evils of steamboat companies or attributing the disaster to God's will. In his 1846 *Steamboat Disasters* book, Warren Lazell reprinted lengthy extracts that ran several pages from the orations of ministers. One was "from an eloquent discourse" delivered at the Brattle Square Church in Boston by the Reverend S.K. Lothrop that mirrored the general public outrage over the disaster that led to blaming the Transportation Company and its employees:

> *The steamboats of Long Island Sound have, until recently, been in general managed with distinguished skill and care, and all necessary, nay, even a scrupulous attention paid to the safety and comfort of the passengers. Of late years, however, the growing competition, and the increased facilities for carrying freight…have…taken from the boats the high character for safety and comfort that once attached to them. They are now, it is said, almost invariably overloaded, the passengers all but crowded out by freight, and their comfort and safety made apparently a secondary consideration.…*
>
> *This awful disaster is to be attributed, either to the selfishness and cupidity of the owners, who, greedy of gain, insisted upon overloading their boat with a dangerous and inflammable freight, or to the culpable carelessness, the utter inattention of the master and officers, in not stowing that freight securely, in not watching over and constantly, with an eagle eye, the condition and safety of the vessel, to which hundreds had entrusted their lives.…It ought to be proclaimed trumpet-tongued, throughout the length and breadth of the land, till it reaches the halls of Congress.*[138]

Rather than focusing on placing blame, the Reverend J.J. Stone of St. Paul's Church in Boston focused on the suffering of those lost: "How terrible at such a moment must have been the awful cry of alarm which broke their feeling of security, and told them that they were within the power of those fearfully opposed elements, flame and flood, fire and frost."[139]

Besides numerous sermons, often reprinted in pamphlets, there were also booklets written by laymen. One published by an anonymous author soon after the disaster carried the tongue-tying title of *A Warning Voice from a Watery Grave!…Or a Solemn Proof of the Uncertainty of Life, and Importance of an Early Preparation for Death! In the Instance of the Melancholy and Untimely Fate of the Much Esteemed and Lamented Miss Sophia W. Wheeler, Who Was One of the Many Unfortunate Victims Who Perished by the Awful Conflagration on Board the Ill-Fated Steamboat Lexington, on Her Passage from New-York to Stonington, January 13,*

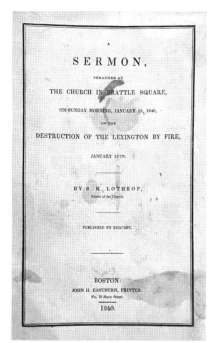
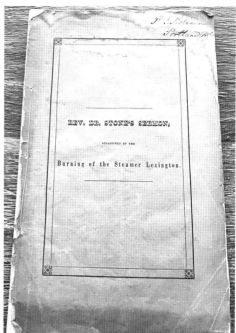

Left: Sermon about the *Lexington* by the Reverend S.K. Lothrop of the Church in Brattle Square in Boston. *Author photo.*

Right: Published sermon on the *Lexington* sinking by the Reverend J.J. Stone of St. Paul's Church in Boston. *Author photo.*

1840. The title aptly describes the contents, which urged readers, especially younger ones, to live a good Christian life before dying.[140]

Biographical information on the passengers and crew had dribbled out in the early reporting. By the time Warren Lazell wrote his book *Steamboat Disasters and Railroad Accidents in the United States to Which Are Appended Accounts of Recent Shipwrecks, Fires at Sea, Thrilling Incidents, Etc.*, in 1846, he was able to compile more information on the more prominent victims, which he delivered at great length and with a healthy dollop of purple prose. "We give them to the reader, as being of particular interest, and as showing the high character and standing of many of those who perished by that awful event," he wrote.[141]

Lazell wrote that Charles Follen, professor of German literature at Harvard College, was born at Romrod in Hesse Darmstadt in 1796. Until 1823, he had been a professor of civil law at the University of Basel in Switzerland.

An illustration of the burning *Lexington* from Warren Lazell's *Steamboat Disasters and Railroad Accidents in the United States to Which Are Appended Accounts of Recent Shipwrecks, Fires at Sea, Thrilling Incidents, etc.* published in 1846.

His animadversions [critical comments] *on the subject of government and law, became displeasing to Austria, a power whose iron and relentless despotism is felt far beyond the limits of her territory. A formal demand was made on the authorities of Basle* [Basel] *that Professor Follen should be delivered up to Austria…and the demand was refused; but afterwards, at the pressing instances of the Austrian government…the authorities of Basle instituted a preliminary process against Professor Follen, in consequence of which he left Switzerland. He first went to France.…In the autumn of 1824…Dr. Follen came out to America. He was soon afterwards employed as a professor of German Literature in Harvard College, where his kindness of manners and varied knowledge made him extremely popular with the students. He subsequently embraced the profession of divinity, and was for a while pastor of a congregation in this city* [Worcester, Massachusetts]. *At the time of his death he resided in Lexington, in Massachusetts, where he had charge of a religious society.…The world had not a firmer, a more ardent, or more consistent friend of human liberty.*[142]

Follen was married to Eliza Cabot of the noted Boston family, and the couple had one child. In 1835, he was hired to be the first preacher at the Free Christian Church in East Lexington, Massachusetts. He was only

The exterior and interior of the Follen Church in East Lexington, Massachusetts. Charles Follen, who in 1835 was hired to be the first preacher at what was then called the Free Christian Church, designed this second edifice for the congregation. He died in the *Lexington* disaster on his way to the dedication of the new octagonal structure. *Tod Thonger photo and Follen.org.*

able to serve for six months and then was replaced by poet and philosopher Ralph Waldo Emerson until Follen returned in 1838. He died in the *Lexington* disaster on his way to the dedication of a new octagonal church that he had designed based on his architectural studies in Germany. A monument to him erected in 1915 on the grounds of the church—now named Follen Church—describes him as "a fearless advocate of liberty and justice."[143]

Mrs. Russell Jarvis—as noted earlier, her first name was not recorded—was the wife of a New Yorker described as either an attorney or editor of the *Evening Tattler*, depending on the source. Lazell wrote that

> when the flames of the boat drove Mrs. Jarvis into the waves, she sprang overboard with one child, and succeeded in reaching a cotton bale. The other child quickly followed, and in attempting to secure her, the distracted mother lost her hold, and the three sank in death together.…Mrs. Jarvis had the greatest aversion to this particular steamboat. But she yielded her objections, as she was attended by two of her relatives. Strange and mysterious providence, that her first venturing where she had the most fear, should be the first step to her watery grave.[144]

Captain Ichabod D. Carver of Plymouth, Massachusetts, was returning from a foreign voyage and was planning to marry as soon as he reached home, Lazell wrote. Captain Benjamin Foster of Providence was returning from a three-year voyage to India. "His wife and children had been anxiously awaiting his arrival for several months, and the dreadful intelligence that reached them of his loss in the *Lexington*, was the first intelligence they received of him."[145]

Boston businessman James Griswold Brown boarded the *Lexington* after writing a friend that "I leave tonight, trusting to the watchful care of my Covenant Shepherd," according to a February 7 article in the *Boston Recorder*.

Some bodies were found or identified long after the initial search had ended. The Sag Harbor *Corrector* reported on February 26 that the body of Boston businessman James Andrew Leach had washed ashore near Old Field Point. The body of Lydia Bates, whose two children were also lost in the disaster, washed ashore near Smithtown in September, the *New York Evening Post* reported on September 23. The body of John Everett Jr. of Boston was later identified through the name of the maker of his boots, the *Providence Evening Press* reported on January 31, 1870.

There is an interesting postscript to the recovery of the four survivors. When pilot Stephen Manchester abandoned the *Lexington*, he had in his

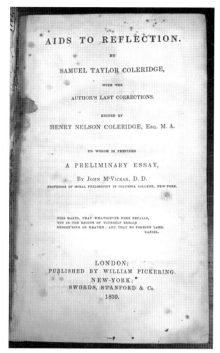
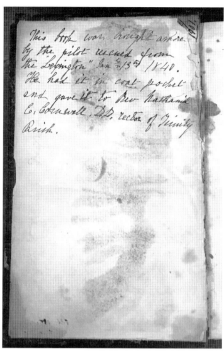

When he abandoned the *Lexington*, Stephen Manchester, the pilot and one of the four survivors, had in his pocket this copy of Samuel Taylor Coleridge's *Aids to Reflection*. The book was donated to the Pequot Library in Southport, Connecticut, in 1901. *Courtesy of Special Collections, Pequot Library, Southport, Connecticut.*

pocket a copy of Samuel Taylor Coleridge's *Aids to Reflection*, published in London the previous year. The book is now in the collection of the Pequot Library in Southport, Connecticut. A handwritten note on the cover states that the book was "Saved from Steamer 'Lexington' burned in Long Island Sound January 13th 1840." A handwritten note inside the cover states that "this book was brought ashore by the pilot rescued from the '*Lexington*' Jan. 13th 1840. He had it in coat pocket and gave it to Rev Nathaniel E. Cornwall, DD, rector of Trinity Parish" in Southport, where Manchester was brought by the sloop *Merchant* after his rescue. Inside the cover on either side of an article about the sinking is another handwritten note: "The original cover on this book was so soaked with salt water that it fell off in a short time and this binding was put on in 1855." On the other side of the article, a note reads: "Presented to 'Pequot Library' of Southport Connecticut by Anna Bedinger Cornwall. 136 West 63rd Street New York. July 24, 1901."

The Burials

The victims of the *Lexington* hailed from as far as New Orleans and England, but a large number lived in Boston, Providence and New York City. The bodies of only fifteen of the passengers and crew members were recovered, present for funeral services and buried under gravestones. Most of the bodies were never found, so memorial monuments were erected to honor some of those victims. Tod Thonger, a Long Island resident who has been researching the *Lexington* since 1983, has identified thirty-one grave or memorial sites of victims and survivors. Six are located in the North Burial Ground in Providence, Rhode Island, the most of any location. That cemetery contains the graves or memorials of three crew members and one passenger and the graves of two surviving crew members.

One of the North Burial Ground memorials is that of Captain George Child. The inscription reads: "Passed from Earth life by the burning of the steamboat *Lexington* in Long Island Sound." Child, who was thirty-six, was survived by his wife, Sarah Marie Beverly Child, and three children.[146]

First Mate Edward Thurber's memorial stone at North Burial Ground reads: "In Memory of Edward Thurber, Lost with the Steamer *Lexington*, Jan. 13, 1840, Aged 51 years." He and his wife, Mehitabel Tucker Thurber (1803–1832), had three children.[147]

The memorial stone for the steamboat's clerk, Jesse Comstock Jr., in North Burial Ground is inscribed: "Erected in Memory of Jesse, age 20 years & seven months. Son of Jesse & Ann Comstock, who perished in Long Island Sound on the evening of Jan. 13, 1840, by the Destruction of the Steam Boat Lexington. The Steam Boat Lexington was destroyed by Fire in Long Island Sound opposite Huntington Lighthouse on the evening of Jan. 13, 1840, by which disaster, 150 Persons, Passengers and Crew, only 4 were saved." Comstock had four siblings. Brother Joseph J. was the steamboat captain hired by the *Lexington*'s owners to search for bodies after the disaster, and brother William was killed in 1854 when his steamer, *Arctic*, sank off Newfoundland after colliding with a French steamer.[148]

The burial of Chief Engineer Cortland Hempstead in the cemetery of the Dutch Reformed Church in downtown Brooklyn was documented in the January 20 issue of the *Long-Island Star*. Hempstead, born in 1809 in New London, Connecticut, lived in Brooklyn with his wife, Margaret.[149] When word reached the city that his body had been recovered on the beach in Southport, David Price and John Stilwell traveled there and brought his remains back to Brooklyn. They arrived at his home on York Street at ten o'clock Saturday night, five days after the fire broke out, and the following afternoon the body was taken to the cemetery "attended…by upwards of four hundred citizens."

The *Star* wrote:

> *We are indebted to Mr. J. Stilwell for the following particulars, which were obtained from Mr. Charles Smith, who is one of the saved and who with Mr. Hempstead, were the last that left the wreck. Mr. Smith was perfectly sensible when he reached the shore, but lies at Southport in a much frozen state. He states that just before the boat went down, Mr. H. jumped from the bows into the water and succeeded in reaching a large fragment of the wreck, upon which he floated to the shore, and Mr. S. at the same time sprang off, and the suction of the boat carried him down—He came up again and succeeded in reaching a piece of the wreck, upon which he floated until picked up. Shortly after the boat went down he lost sight of Mr. Hempstead, and did not see him again until the body was found in a reclining posture upon the piece of wreck on which he first saw him. He thinks that from appearances, Mr. Hempstead could not have been dead half an hour when found.*
>
> *Mr. Hempstead was 33 years of age and has spent the greater part of his life in the city* [Brooklyn, then a separate city]. *He was much esteemed by all who knew him, and his sudden departure from the world is deeply lamented.*

In the 1850s, the Dutch Reformed Church sold its property. Those buried there, including Hempstead, were relocated to the Dutch Reformed Church Lot in the famous and fashionable Green-Wood Cemetery in Brooklyn, according to the cemetery historian, Jeffrey I. Richman. Hempstead's gravestone features an engraving of the *Lexington* ablaze. Over the years, the distinctive headstone in the Cedar Dell section sank into the ground, making it impossible to read the inscription below the burning steamboat. In 2009, the cemetery's restoration crew lifted the stone and reset it so visitors can now read the full inscription for the "Late Chief Engineer of the Steamer Lexington."[150]

The body of passenger Philo Upson, a successful thirty-nine-year-old businessman and quarry co-owner from Egremont, Massachusetts, is believed to have been the first recovered on the Long Island shore. He was buried in Mount Everett Cemetery in Egremont. The inscription on his obelisk monument states:

> *The Quarry which gave him so many while he lived, gives this last block to perpetuate his memory. He perished with one hundred & forty fellow*

Gravestone of Cortland Hempstead, "Late Chief Engineer of the Steamer *Lexington*," at Green-Wood Cemetery in Brooklyn. *Courtesy of Jeffrey I. Richman.*

passengers at the burning of the steamboat Lexington *in Long Island Sound on the night of 13 Jan. 1840. A catastrophe which brought mourning into many families and spreading all over society. Energetic, upright, benevolent in all the relations of life, exemplary in business, imbued with the spirit of the age. While preparing to execute large and honorable plans, he was suddenly removed, leaving the record of his virtues more indelibly engraved upon the minds of numerous friends, than this inscription upon the marble.*

According to *The Upson Family in America*, compiled by the Upson Family Association of America in 1940, Philo Upson was born on June 10, 1803, in Otis, Massachusetts. He was a member of the sixth generation of his family in America. He was married on May 1, 1828, to Sarah Curtiss of Sheffield, Massachusetts, who died on May 19, 1877, in South Egremont. They had three children. "Philo Upson early showed an aptitude for business, but his life was cut short," the family history said. "*The Berkshire Courier* of January 25, 1840, says that he had been for several years extensively engaged in the marble business, furnishing the material for Girard College in Philadelphia. He left for that city; returned to New York and took passage on the steamboat *Lexington* for Boston….Mr. Upson…employed a large number of persons in his various operations and disbursed large sums of money. He was high-minded and enterprising, his word or his bond being considered the same." Besides the quarry, Upson owned a woolen factory, plaster mill, sawmill, blacksmith shop, wagon shop, eighty-eight acres of woodland, three small farms and a brick house on two and a half acres where he lived. His widow had to move into a smaller house next door, where she lived until her death, and the original residence became the Olde Egremont Tavern.[151]

There is a memorial stone for Jonathan Porter Felt Jr., a twenty-six-year-old merchant from Salem, Massachusetts, in that community's Harmony Grove Cemetery. It is inscribed, "In Memory of J. Porter Felt, Jr. Son of Jonathan P. and Margaret Felt, Born Nov. 1813 and was lost by the burning of the Steamboat *Lexington* on Long Island Sound on the night of Jan. 13, 1840." Felt and his wife, Ann Baker Kennedy (1787–1863), had no children.[152]

A memorial for fifty-five-year-old Captain Theophilus Smith of Dartmouth, Massachusetts, was erected in the Methodist Cemetery in that community. The stone reads: "Lost on board Steam Boat *Lexington*." He and his wife, Esther Nickerson Smith (1785–1853), had two children.[153]

The gravestone for *Lexington* passenger George Swan and his brother Albert at Green-Wood Cemetery in Brooklyn. *Courtesy of Jeffrey I. Richman.*

George and Albert Swan of Columbus, Ohio, were the sons of Gustavus Swan, a prominent lawyer and Ohio Supreme Court judge. Both attended Harvard College. George died on his way there aboard the *Lexington*, and his body was not recovered. Albert became ill and died five years later in New York, also en route to Harvard. They share a headstone in Green-Wood Cemetery in Brooklyn.[154]

Near the entrance to South Cemetery in Belchertown, Massachusetts, a large stone marks the graves of two members of the Walker family. The inscription on the lower half reads, "Harrison J.O. Walker, Perished by the destruction of the Steamer Lexington on Long Island Sound, Jan. 13, 1840, age 18." The local *Hampshire Gazette* reported, "We are pained to learn that a young man by the name of Walker, who has a brother in this town, and whose parents live in Belchertown, was lost in the steamboat *Lexington*."[155] (A full list of the thirty-one known grave and memorial sites is in the appendix.)

THE NEWS COVERAGE CONTINUES

Stories about the *Lexington* continued to appear in the newspapers for months after the last burials or memorial services. The *New York Evening Post* reported on June 26 that the wife of Alexander H. Fowler, an organ maker from the city, had received a letter in handwriting similar to her husband's claiming he had survived on a bale of cotton for three days before being picked up by a vessel headed for Mobile, Alabama, where he had been hospitalized for the previous five months. The newspaper followed up several days later to say that the letter was a hoax "written for the poor motive of adding to the trouble of his widow."

Even when the newspapers had nothing new to report and had moved on to other events, the story of the *Lexington* did not fade from memory because it began to be a subject in books.

In *Steamboat Disasters*, published in 1840, S.A. Howland wrote floridly: "The lurid light of the blazing wreck shone far over the cold and dreary waste of waters....Human beings were floating around in every direction,—some were yet living, but more had ceased to be,—some were struggling to gain a fragment or bale of cotton,—while others, in happy unconsciousness, were sinking into the cold flood of death."[156]

In his *Steamboat Disasters* book published in 1846, Warren Lazell wrote extensively about the disaster six years earlier in sometimes purple prose: "The boat drifted about on the sea at the mercy of wind and tide, while the flames were sweeping over her from bow to stern. The scene that ensued was appalling, and baffles all attempt at description."

THE SURVIVORS AFTER THE DISASTER

After the sinking of the *Lexington*, Second Mate David Crowley and fireman Charles B. Smith worked together again on New Jersey Steam Navigation Company vessels, and they would play a role in another steamboat disaster. That occurred in April 1866 when the *City of Norwich* collided with the schooner *Gen. S. van Vliet* near Huntington, Long Island, shortly before four o'clock on a hazy morning. The schooner "struck the *City of Norwich* just forward [of] the port bow with great force, tearing her timbers and knocking a large hole in her side, through which the water rushed into the vessel in large quantities," the *New England Farmer* of Boston reported. The impact almost cut the steamboat in half and ignited a fire from the furnaces, forcing passengers and crew to jump into Long Island Sound and cling to bales and boxes. The steamboat *Electra*, which was following the *City of Norwich* on the route from New York to Boston, came to their rescue. Crowley was serving as the first mate with Smith as chief engineer. They and the other officers supervised the launching of four boats from their vessel.

> *Their labor was a perilous one, but the brave men and the boats persevered in their efforts to save the struggling men and women. The boats were urged among floating wreck[age], surrounded by flames, which burned many of the rescuers, and in a short time they succeeded in taking from the water and bringing on board the* Electra, *lying a little distance off, the great greater part of the crew and passengers. The steamer had some fifty persons aboard, of whom forty were saved.*[157]

Pilot Stephen Manchester, who lived in Providence at the time of the disaster, returned to working on steamboats. By 1846, he was the captain of the *Rhode Island* operating between New York and Stonington. The *Boston Daily Bee* ran an item on October 17 of that year that the large vessel was unequaled for its speed, safety and comfort. Manchester remained in Providence with his wife, Rhoda, until her death in 1849, which was reported in the April 30 edition of the city's *Manufacturers' and Farmers' Journal.* He then moved far from Long Island Sound to Chicago, where he died in 1859, according to the *Boston Traveler* of June 24.

The only surviving passenger, Captain Chester Hillard, who previously had served as master of the packet ship *Mississippi* for the Collins Packet Line in New Orleans, returned there after the disaster. He became the New Orleans agent for a New York City packet line in 1850. He remained in the Crescent City until the Civil War, when he returned to Connecticut.

Hillard was born on November 26, 1815, in Preston, Connecticut. He and his wife, Julia A. Barker, who died in 1875, had two children. When Hillard died at age fifty-two, he was buried in Yantic Cemetery in Norwich, Connecticut. His headstone reads: "Captain Chester Hillard—the only surviving passenger of the ill fated Lexington. November 26, 1815, March 21, 1868."[158]

His obituary on the front page of the New Orleans *Times-Picayune* of April 12, 1868, praised him for demonstrating "winning social qualities and sterling virtues, which commanded the friendship, respect and affection of a large circle of acquaintances and relations."

At some point, Second Mate David Crowley began working for the Providence and Stonington Steamship Company and became a captain.[159] Because of his notoriety and financial status, Crowley was the subject of an elegant portrait painted twelve years after the sinking by Samuel Lovett Waldo and William Jewett with vignettes of the burning steamboat and Crowley on a cotton bale in the background. It is in the collection of the Rhode Island Historical Society in Providence.[160]

On August 22, 1881, the *Providence Daily Journal* reprinted a short item about Crowley from the *Boston Traveler*. It described him as a "veteran of Long Island Sound navigation, having commenced service in 1832." After recounting his survival from

Captain Chester Hillard was the only passenger on the *Lexington* to survive. He is buried in Yantic Cemetery in Norwich, Connecticut. *Tod Thonger photo.*

Left: Portrait of *Lexington* second mate David Crowley, one of the four survivors, painted twelve years after the disaster by Samuel Lovett Waldo and William Jewett with vignettes of the burning steamboat and Crowley on a cotton bale in the background. *Courtesy of the Rhode Island Historical Society. RHi X 17 3429.*

Right: The broken headstone for *Lexington*'s Second Mate David Crowley in North Burial Ground in Providence, Rhode Island. *Author photo.*

the *Lexington*, the newspaper wrote, "That Mr. Crowley has become a favorite with the passengers over the Sound is not to be wondered at. His urbanity and courtesy have won him hosts of friends among the traveling public. More than this, he makes no distinction, and the poorest emigrant on board the steamer *Narragansett* receives as much attention from him as the occupant of the highest-priced stateroom."

Crowley worked on steamboats for fifty-three years after the loss of the *Lexington*. A story headlined "Mr. Crowley's Retirement" ran in the *Providence Daily Journal* on January 19, 1893. "Mr. David Crowley, who has been employed on steamers connected with the Stonington line for many years, has relinquished his position, and retired from steamboat service," the article begins. It then recounts the demise of the *Lexington*, noting that Crowley was serving as second mate and baggage master, "the two positions being then filled by one man." After surviving the sinking, "the terrors of that experience have never been effaced from Mr. Crowley's memory, and he can but seldom be persuaded to recite the circumstances connected therewith, as it is a painful subject for him to contemplate." The story noted that "the bale of cotton that served as his life preserver he retained in his possession for many years, but during the War of the Rebellion [Civil War] cotton advanced to a fabulous price, and he was persuaded to sell it. During recent years, Mr. Crowley has served as baggage master, running between Boston and New York via the steamboat train and the boat."[161]

Crowley had another brush with death in an accident only two months after he retired. The *Boston Journal* reported on March 2, 1893, that Crowley was a passenger on an overnight train on the New York, New Haven and Hartford Railroad when it collided at 5:25 a.m. with another train in Norwood, Rhode Island. A child was killed, and half a dozen other passengers were injured. Crowley was sitting in the same car as the child who died, but he suffered only a cut by his eye that required a few stitches. The newspaper wrote that "the man who lived 48 hours floating on a bale of cotton, and thus escaped death in the burning *Lexington*, would seem to be proof against any ordinary railroad accident."

Crowley died on November 17, 1900, and joined George Child and others from the *Lexington* in Providence's North Burial Ground. Unfortunately, his headstone is broken into several pieces lying on the ground. The author of this book is trying to organize a fundraising campaign to have it restored. Sadly, the cemetery records show Crowley's last residence was Butler Hospital, a Providence institution for the mentally ill. The burial records show no information about him having married.[162]

On November 9, 1900, the *Journal* ran a short legal notice with the heading: "Municipal Court of the city of Providence, October 25, 1900." It stated that a petition had been made by David B. Hall of Providence to be appointed guardian of Crowley's estate.[163]

An article in the *Providence Daily Journal* on January 14, 1896, marking the fifty-sixth anniversary of the fire, noted that Charles B. Smith had brought a picture of the steamboat before the fire to the newspaper office, where it was being displayed in an office window. At that point, Smith was living in South Seekonk and was seventy-five years old "and quite vigorous. Until about five years ago he was engineer in charge of the pumps at the Hope reservoir, where he had been for over 10 years."[164]

The *Daily Journal* printed a story about Smith on January 31, 1901, marking his eighty-first birthday. Under the headline of "The Last Survivor" and subhead of "East Providence Man Was on Steamer *Lexington* When It Burned," the story said that

> *Charles B. Smith, who resides at 202 Summit street, East Providence, attained his 81st birthday Sunday. He is the last survivor of the crew and*

THE LAST SURVIVOR.

East Providence Man Was on Steamer Lexington When It Burned.

Charles B. Smith, who resides at 202 Summit street, East Providence, attained his 51st birthday Sunday. He is the last survivor of the crew and passengers on the ill-fated steamer Lexington, which was burned on Long Island Sound Jan. 13, 1840. He was rated as a fireman, but was an oiler to the chief engineer. But four persons escaped the disaster, and he believes that he is the last survivor. Until last winter there was another, a man named Colwell, but Mr. Smith thinks he has died.

Mr. Smith was also a "Forty-niner."

CHARLES B. SMITH.
The last survivor of the burning of steamer Lexington.

Above: Article about surviving *Lexington* crew member Charles B. Smith in the *Providence Daily Journal* on January 3, 1901.

Right: Surviving crew member Charles B. Smith's grave in the North Burial Ground in Providence, Rhode Island. *Author photo.*

passengers on the ill-fated steamer Lexington, *which was burned on Long Island Sound Jan. 13, 1840. He was rated as a fireman, but was an oiler to the chief engineer. But four persons escaped the disaster, and he believed that he is the last survivor. Until last winter, there was another, a man named Colwell* [Crowley], *but Mr. Smith thinks he has died.*

Mr. Smith was also a "Forty-niner." His principal occupation has been that of a steamboat engineer, and he served in that capacity in the South during the Civil War and many years afterward, but was 11 years engineer at the Hope Pumping Station of the city. Mr. Smith appears to be in quite good health. He retains his physical and mental capacities in a great degree. Last winter he was a great sufferer from pneumonia, grip and pleurisy, which came in succession, and, although weakened by the sickness of that time, no one would suppose him to have arrived at the age of four score years.

Smith, who was born on December 29, 1820, in Norwich, Connecticut, died on November 3, 1905, at age eighty-four. He is buried at the North Burial Ground in Providence, the same cemetery where Captain George Child was buried sixty-five years earlier and David Crowley was buried in 1900. He was married to Hannah D. Handy (1818–1896) and then Elener L. Read.[165]

On November 12, the *Providence Sunday Journal* noted the passing of Smith in its summary of activities by fraternal groups. Under the Knights of Pythias, it said, "The death of Brother Charles B. Smith was reported and the funeral benefit ordered paid. The lodge attended the funeral and with the Odd Fellows held service at the grave."

Long after the sinking of the *Lexington*, the four survivors continued to make news. But the loss of the vessel was immortalized to a much greater degree by the work of lithographers who seared the image of the burning vessel into the public imagination.

6

IMAGES OF THE DISASTER

I f people in 1840 and following years had a vivid sense of what the *Lexington* ablaze looked like, it was because of young lithographer Nathaniel Currier and his groundbreaking image *Awful Conflagration of the Steam Boat LEXINGTON in Long Island Sound on Monday Evening, January 13th 1840, by Which Melancholy Occurrence, Over 100 PERSONS PERISHED.*

Currier—who would later famously partner with James Merritt Ives to create the firm of Currier & Ives—collaborated with the editors at the New York *Sun*, the city's largest daily newspaper, to produce an image of the burning steamboat so the newspaper could print special "extra" editions featuring the lithograph. Some of them were hand-colored by women working for Currier, each adding a different watercolor tint assembly-line fashion. It was possibly the first illustrated newspaper extra edition in American history. The *Sun* printed the first image of the fire three days after the disaster. It was not credited to any artist, and it may or may not have been created by Currier's firm. The first lithograph definitively linked to him appeared in the newspaper ten days after the sinking. And after the *Sun* ran several versions over many days, Currier began printing his own hand-colored copies, which sold widely.

"The signal innovation in coverage of the *Lexington* debacle was the creation of timely visual representations," Cynthia A. Kierner wrote in her 2019 book *Inventing Disaster*. The at least fifteen versions of the *Sun* extras "were among the earliest near-contemporaneous depictions of newsworthy events, as well as the first representation of a steamboat explosion

Nathaniel Currier's Manhattan lithography firm produced the famous image *Awful Conflagration of the Steam Boat LEXINGTON in Long Island Sound on Monday Evening, January 13th 1840, by Which Melancholy Occurrence, Over 100 PERSONS PERISHED* for the New York *Sun*. It was one of the images used to illustrate a breaking news story "extra" edition for the first time in an American daily newspaper, and it made Currier famous. *Courtesy of James Brust.*

immediately after it happened. These images fueled fascination with the *Lexington* disaster among the general public. One New Yorker reported that, more than a week after the [fire], 'the sensation is prolonged....Nothing else is talked of in society.'"[166]

Genoa Shepley, a scholar of nineteenth-century representations of disaster, stated in a 2015 article that "while the disaster sent a wave of trepidation across America, it augured a brilliant future for the fledgling printing firm of N. Currier." His *Awful Conflagration* "appeared in record time and was delivered through the uncommon distribution mode of a news extra. It propelled him to national prominence."[167]

"Disaster prints worked in tandem with representations of fires and shipwrecks in other visual formats, which were increasingly accessible to a paying public," Kierner observed. Currier had begun producing disaster scenes in 1835 with two lithographs of New York's Great Fire, which besides being printed on paper were even reproduced on dinner plates made in England for export to the United States. That fire image and another by Currier of the 1837 shipwreck of the *Mexico* on the South Shore of Long

Island were turned into dioramas where audiences viewed a succession of large images accompanied by music and sound effects. After the *Lexington* fire, the New England Museum in Boston exhibited a "panorama of this awful tragedy." "Disaster stories and their visual representations were part of a larger popular culture of sensationalism, which, beginning with the emergence of the so-called penny press in the 1830s, pervaded the antebellum era," Kierner stated.[168]

Currier's images of disasters "resonated with America's growing middle-class," Shepley wrote. They

> *managed a complex set of psychological and cultural tensions to appeal to the sensibilities of a broad swath of antebellum viewers. Comprising some of the first lithographs on newsworthy subjects disseminated in the United States on a mass scale, these "marketable" disasters portrayed large-scale events and often featured a modern technology or system abruptly and dramatically undermined by primal natural forces. These prints gave an unprecedented visual immediacy to incidents that loom large in the public imagination, at a price that made them widely accessible....Simultaneously more spectacular, imaginative, and subtle than the newspaper reports of the same events, more immediate and local than "high-art" renderings, and more enduring than theatrical performances, these first Currier lithographs gave the viewers a space in which to contemplate the vicissitudes of fortune.[169]*

Nathaniel Currier (1813–1888) lived in a time of rapid change. "His own life trajectory and those of many of his associates arced across one of the most economically, socially, and politically volatile periods in American history—one marked by financial downturns, military conflicts, and massive physical and class dislocations as the tottering republic found its balance and matured into a modern industrial society," Kierner wrote. "Currier's seventy-five years on this earth also witnessed the advent of technological marvels—steam-powered ships and railroads—that remodeled the topography of the country and radically altered the flow of people within it. Such transformations brought with them the possibility of catastrophic conflict and sudden, grisly death on a grand scale. Visible evidence of this instability frequently recurs in the more than seven thousand images of the firm of Currier & Ives over its 70-year existence."[170]

The upheaval and instability were in full view when Currier was born in Roxbury, Massachusetts, during the War of 1812. At age fifteen, he became an apprentice at Pendleton's Lithography in Boston, one of the first such

Right: Lithographer Nathaniel Currier, whose image of the *Lexington* ablaze made him famous. *Courtesy of Jeffrey I. Richman.*

Below: Nathaniel Currier's first disaster print: *Ruins of the Merchant's Exchange N.Y. after the Destructive Conflagration of Decbr. 16 & 17, 1835;* N. Currier's Press. *New York Public Library.*

firms in the country. He trained there for three years with fellow apprentice John Henry Bufford, who would collaborate on Currier's initial successful efforts. Currier and Bufford both moved to New York City and set up shops, in 1834 and 1835, respectively. Currier's attempts at two partnerships were unsuccessful, so after a year he began his own company when he was twenty-two. Initially, he was solely a job printer, producing work such as letterheads for clients, until he began turning out disaster images.[171]

Early on, lithography[172] was a collaborative business involving joint work by employees of a single shop and even competitors. "The individual contributions of a draftsman, printer, publisher, and distributor are most often impossible to distinguish," Shepley wrote. To make it more difficult to determine Currier's own efforts, few of his business records have survived. Currier hired or commissioned other artists to produce the prints that he published under his name. And rather than take a financial risk, he would often turn to John Disturnell, a writer, printer and book dealer known for publishing guidebooks, to distribute his work.[173]

When a large fire destroyed more than thirteen acres of New York's business district on December 16, 1835, the year that "N. Currier" opened his office at 1 Wall Street, the young entrepreneur saw an opportunity. He collaborated with Bufford and Disturnell to issue *Ruins of the Merchant's Exchange N.Y. after the Destructive Conflagration of Dec. 16 & 17, 1835* within days of the blaze. It was initially printed in black-and-white and then in a hand-colored edition.[174] "While newspapers were capable of incorporating rough woodcut imagery in pace with the news cycle," Shepley wrote, "their editors greatly favored text and only used small illustrations, if any. 'Hence, the dazzling speed of Currier's presses created a sensation.' This print—one of his first forays into original subject matter—reportedly sold in the thousands and helped to establish Currier's local reputation." The prints, which did not include Currier's name, would have been priced at four to seven dollars in today's money, making them easily affordable for middle-class customers. The idea was to attract a broad audience that would hang them in bars, firehouses and other public gathering spots but probably not the parlors of homes given the disturbing subject matter. The marketing strategy is evidenced by the sales slogan employed later by Currier & Ives: "Popular Cheap Prints."[175]

When Currier started out, the only newspapers in the city were expensive subscription-only publications geared to upper-class readership. That changed with the introduction of the "penny press" newspapers that were hawked on the street and focused on emotional human-interest stories. One

Top: An early masthead of the New York *Sun*, which was founded in 1833 and used a lithograph of the *Lexington* on fire in one of the first illustrated newspaper extra editions in 1840. *Courtesy of Stephen Goldman.*

Bottom: Nathaniel Currier's *Dreadful Wreck of the Mexico on Hempstead Beach, January 2ⁿᵈ, 1837— As Now Exhibiting at Hanington Dioramas—Perished in All—115 Souls*. It was Currier's first maritime disaster lithograph. *Public domain.*

of the first was the New York *Sun*, established in 1833. The *Daily Transcript* came soon afterward, followed by the *Herald* in 1835. By that time, the first two newspapers were selling about ten thousand copies a day.[176]

The first print of a shipwreck to bear Currier's name was the *Dreadful Wreck of the Mexico on Hempstead Beach. January 2ⁿᵈ, 1837* produced that year.[177] It depicts the wreck on the southern shore of Long Island of a ship carrying Irish immigrants and other poor residents of the British Isles from Liverpool to New York. It was carrying 111 passengers and 12 crew when it ran aground in a snowstorm off Long Beach Island. Only 8 survived—the

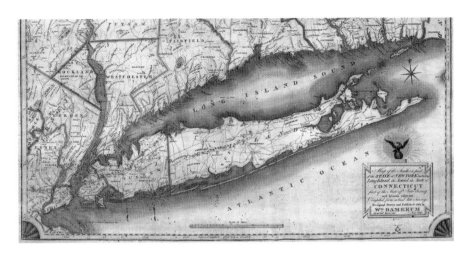

Bottom portion of "Map of the southern part of the state of New York including Long Island, the Sound, the state of Connecticut, part of the state of New Jersey, and islands adjacent compiled from actual late surveys," prepared by William Damerum and Peter Maverick in 1819. The *Lexington* sank northwest of Port Jefferson. *Library of Congress.*

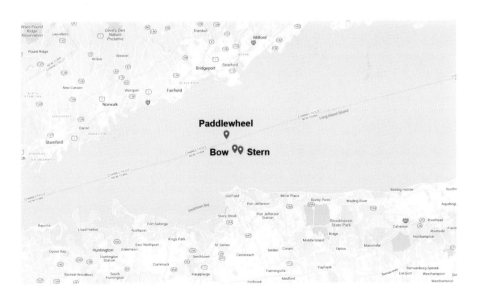

The final locations of the bow (*lower left*), stern (*lower right*) and surviving paddlewheel (*top*). There is no trace of the second paddlewheel. *Courtesy of Ben Roberts.*

John Ferguson Weir's painting *The Gun Foundry* depicting the West Point Foundry in Cold Spring on the Hudson River, which made the steam engine for the *Lexington*. *Courtesy of Putnam History Museum.*

The anonymous lithograph of the burning steamboat printed by the New York *Sun* in its extra editions before the paper substituted Nathaniel Currier's famous image. *Courtesy of James Brust.*

Left: The New York *Sun* extra edition featuring the lithograph produced by the firm of Nathaniel Currier, one of the first times an American daily newspaper illustrated a breaking news event in an extra edition. *Courtesy of Stephen Goldman.*

Below: *Awful Conflagration of the Steam Boat Lexington* printed by D.W. Kellogg & Co. and published by Morgan & Ferre, 1840. *Connecticut Historical Society collection 2003.263.0.*

Awful Conflagration of the Steam Boat Lexington in Long Island Sound lithograph by an unknown publisher. *Author photo.*

An unsigned lithograph of the *Lexington* ablaze. *Author photo.*

Top: A miniature portrait of *Lexington* captain George Child probably painted in the 1820s by an unidentified artist. *Connecticut Historical Society collection 1972.11.1.*

Bottom: Portrait of *Lexington* second mate David Crowley, one of the four survivors, painted twelve years after the disaster by Samuel Lovett Waldo and William Jewett with vignettes of the burning steamboat and Crowley on a cotton bale in the background. *Courtesy of the Rhode Island Historical Society. RHi X 17 3429.*

Portrait of the Reverend Dr. Charles Follen, a Harvard professor and antislavery activist hired as the first preacher at the Free Christian Church in East Lexington, Massachusetts. He died in the *Lexington* disaster on his way to the dedication of a new church. A monument to him was erected in 1915 on the grounds of the church—now named Follen Church. *Follen.org.*

Pilot Stephen Manchester had a copy of Samuel Taylor Coleridge's *Aids to Reflection* in his pocket when he abandoned the burning *Lexington*. After he was rescued and taken to Southport, Connecticut, he gave the waterlogged volume to Nathaniel E. Cornwall, rector of Trinity Parish. It was donated to the Pequot Library in Southport in 1901. *Courtesy of Special Collections, Pequot Library, Southport, Connecticut.*

Memorial stone for Captain George Child in North Burial Ground in Providence, Rhode Island. *Author photo.*

Top: Chief Engineer Cortland Hempstead is buried in Green-Wood Cemetery in Brooklyn. His gravestone features an engraving of the steamboat ablaze. After the headstone sank into the ground over the years, in 2009 the cemetery's restoration crew reset the stone so visitors can now read the full inscription for the "Late Chief Engineer of the Steamer Lexington." *Courtesy of Jeffrey I. Richman.*

Bottom: The memorial stone for *Lexington* clerk Jesse Comstock Jr., whose body was not recovered, in North Burial Ground in Providence. *Tod Thonger photo.*

The body of passenger Charles Lee of Boston was not recovered, but a memorial stone was erected for him in the Lee Family Cemetery in Barre, Massachusetts. *Tod Thonger photo.*

The memorial stone for passenger John Brown of Boston, whose body was not recovered, at Mount Auburn Cemetery in Cambridge, Massachusetts. *Tod Thonger photo.*

Above: Captain Chester Hillard was the only passenger on the *Lexington* to survive. He is buried in Yantic Cemetery in Norwich, Connecticut. *Tod Thonger photo.*

Left: Jonathan Porter Felt Jr. was a twenty-six-year-old merchant from Salem, Massachusetts. While his body was never found, a memorial stone was placed in that community's Harmony Grove Cemetery. *Tod Thonger photo.*

Top: The primitive diving bell used by Mark W. Davis of Newark, New Jersey, in salvage attempts on the *Lexington* in 1843 and 1850. It is now on display at Library Park in Harrison, New Jersey. *Tod Thonger photo.*

Bottom: Author Clive Cussler on a dive boat by the Throgs Neck Bridge at the western end of Long Island Sound in an undated photo. Cussler put together the 1983 expedition that rediscovered the wreck of the *Lexington* after 133 years. *Courtesy of Stephen Goldman.*

Above: Close-up photo of the *Lexington* taken by diver Robert Wass during the 1983 expedition that rediscovered the shipwreck. The lack of ambient light and overall poor visibility usually found at the site are apparent. *Courtesy of Robert Wass*.

Left: Robert Wass at his Long Island home with a piece of *Lexington* wreckage that he recovered in a dive subsequent to Clive Cussler's 1983 expedition. *Author photo*.

Opposite: Diver Robert Wass on the dive boat after recovering a piece of burnt wood from the *Lexington* in 1983. *Courtesy of Stephen Goldman*.

Top: Smaller artifacts recovered by diver Robert Wass in the 1983 expedition laid out on the deck of the dive boat. *Courtesy of Stephen Goldman.*

Bottom: Ben Roberts on his boat with the side-scan sonar equipment he used to make images of the *Lexington* in 2020. *Courtesy of Ben Roberts.*

Photographs of the shipwreck taken in 2013 by diver John Beninati, formerly of Connecticut and now a North Carolina resident, illustrate the low ambient light and poor visibility typical in the depths of Long Island Sound. *Copyright John Beninati.*

Above: Side-scan images of the stern and bow of the *Lexington* made in 2020 by Ben Roberts below a painting of the vessel. *Courtesy of Ben Roberts*.

Left: Side-scan image of one of the *Lexington* paddlewheels made by Ben Roberts in 2020. There is no trace of the second paddlewheel. *Courtesy of Ben Roberts*.

captain, 4 other crew members and 3 passengers.[178] The caption under the image, rarely mentioned in the literature on Currier & Ives, notes that it was drawn "on the spot by artist H. Sewell" and was "Exhibiting at Hanington's Dioramas." This was a departure from Currier's earlier efforts, which were published simultaneously with penny press newspaper stories. This one was also part of a theatrical performance that began only a week after the disaster at Hanington's "Dioramic Institute," which was located inside the City Saloon on Broadway and was one of the commercial moving dioramas of its day. For a price under fifty cents, audiences could experience scenes staged in the form of large paintings on screens that were attached to giant rollers and unfurled past the audience accompanied by narration, music and sound effects.[179]

The publisher of record for the *Mexico* shipwreck lithograph was Benjamin H. Day, owner of the New York *Sun*, who was known for his unorthodox tactics for raising circulation. The collaboration with Currier set the stage for the far more famous image of the *Lexington* ablaze in 1840. "This print marks an evolution in Currier's understanding of his audience and in his marketing techniques," Shepley wrote. "It entered into circulation in an unprecedented manner for a lithograph and represents a new threshold in Currier's developing sense of how to balance sensation and decorum."[180]

The origin legend for the *Lexington* lithograph is that Currier happened to be in the *Sun* office when news of the disaster on the Sound was received. But lithograph historian James Brust, a Currier & Ives collector for almost fifty years, told the author of this book that "I am not aware of any primary source evidence that it is true." In any case, the paper's owner at the time, Moses Beach, quickly realized the significance of the story and made plans to capitalize on it. An anonymous artist created an initial lithographic image printed in the first extra editions of the newspaper. Then Currier assigned artist William K. Hewitt to depict the scene, and the newspaper and Currier turned it into a best-selling, iconic image.[181] Shepley described why it became so famous:

> *If the* Dreadful Wreck of the Mexico *rolled by enthralled audiences for more than two months* [at Hanington's Dioramas], *the* Awful Conflagration of the Steam Boat Lexington in Long Island Sound *trumped the former shipwreck on several fronts. Also in the dead of winter, the* Lexington *disaster involved a massive fire that demanded of its 140* [actually up to 146] *victims a terrible choice between burning on board or freezing to death in the icy waters of Long Island Sound. It was*

sparked by the incautious choice, driven by profit motives, of transporting a flammable commodity—cotton—too near the hot smokestack of a ship carrying passengers and by the fitting of blowers on the boilers that overheated the stacks. [This was not proven by the inquest testimony.] *It sent to the bottom of the sea the very popular vessel—of revolutionary speed and design—personally commissioned by rising transportation magnate Cornelius Vanderbilt and launched only five years before. The grand 205-foot* Lexington, *built at a price tag of $75,000, went down in a blaze in the middle of a nationwide economic depression.*[182]

The *Lexington* disaster shares some similarities with the early twentieth-century loss of the *Titanic* in the depressed economic conditions of the time, the failure to provide sufficient lifeboats for all aboard and the huge amount of newspaper coverage of the sinking.

When news of the tragedy reached Manhattan two days after the sinking, the *Sun*, a morning newspaper, printed an afternoon extra edition containing the first description of the event. It was illustrated with a small woodcut of the *Lexington* underway in better times. On January 16, the regular edition of the *Sun*, along with the other city newspapers, carried updated reports of the disaster.

But the *Sun* also printed a striking message:

We have, in the hands of a skillful artist, and will be prepared to issue from our counter, about 3 o'clock this afternoon, an accurate and elegantly executed LITHOGRAPHIC REPRESENTATION OF THE DESTRUCTION OF THE STEAMER LEXINGTON, *the dreadful particulars of which appear in our paper this morning. The names of the officers and crew of the unfortunate boat, and of as many of her ill-fated passages as can be obtained, will accompany the Lithograph and form a part of it.*[183]

The morning edition of Friday, January 17, confirms that the illustrated news extra had been printed the previous day.[184] But lithograph historians were unable to find a copy of that first edition until early in 2022, when one of the most prominent of those historians, James Brust, located one of them, he told the author.

The Saturday, January 18 edition provides more information on the lithograph:

The Lithographic Representation of the heartrending scene described by Capt. Hilliard, which we published on Thursday, together with a list of the victims, has been very generally sought for, and continues to be demanded nearly as fast as it is possible to print them. The list has been revised and corrected as fast as diligent inquiry has enabled us to do so, and is now unquestionably as full and accurate as it is likely it will ever be possible to make it.[185]

While the headlines and layout of the type went through several transformations in the days after the anonymous lithograph was first published, the illustration did not initially. The image in the Friday edition on January 17 was similar to the one that became famous but shows the fire during daytime and is less dramatic and less skillfully done. It does not name the artist or lithographer, and there is no map of Long Island Sound. By Tuesday, January 21, the page described the beginning of the official inquest.

On Thursday morning, January 23, the newspaper published the following notice:

We shall, this morning, publish a Lithographic Representation, and letter-press history of the dreadful disaster of the Lexington, *which will far surpass any thing of the kind yet presented. The plate represents the calamity as a night scene—which it, in reality, was—and is executed with much more accuracy and finish than any others. On the same plate is also a chart* [nautical map] *of Long Island and the Sound, with the localities all accurately laid down, as also the precise spot on which the disaster occurred. The chart, and the scene of destruction and death, will be colored on a large quantity of this superior publication, and will greatly add to their value to purchasers. The account of the disaster, and the particulars connected with it, together with a list of the sufferers, as far as they had become known, up to last evening, will be printed on the same sheet—the whole forming a most valuable publication.*[186]

The Thursday, January 23 edition, besides including the map of Long Island Sound, had the different image and below it stated that it was "Drawn by W.K. Hewitt" and was credited to "N. Currier Lith. & Pub. 2 Spruce St. N.Y." Over the next few days, the newspaper made minor variations to the Long Island map and lettering.[187]

Then on Tuesday, January 28, the newspaper printed the following notice:

It is now two weeks since the dreadful calamity of the Lexington *in the Sound swept from life to death 150* [actually up to 146] *human beings, and made mourners of thousands; and the excitement which is produced in our community is but little allayed as yet. Between twelve and thirteen thousand of our lithograph and letterpress histories of that awful disaster have been taken from our counter by eager purchasers, and the sales of them daily amount to hundreds. But few are left for sale, and those who are still unprovided will do well to supply themselves without further delay, as we shall be obliged to suspend the sale of them in a few days, owing to the press of other business, which has been suffering on account of the great encroachment upon our ever-occupied time, occasioned by this popular, though melancholy publication.*[188]

When the *Sun* ceased running the Currier image, the lithographer carried on independently. Sheets were printed that omit the "The Extra Sun" headline and "Pub. at Sun Office" credit line but still contain the image, the list of victims and Hillard's testimony at the inquest. Currier's name now appears under the right bottom corner of the lithograph and at the bottom of the text, showing that he is now the publisher of the page. Several variations followed, including one that states at the end of the text just above Currier's name: "W. Applegate Printer, 17 Ann Street," indicating that he printed the text for Currier. Another variation revises the title below the lithograph to read "120 **PERSONS PERISHED**" and the map disappears. Eventually, there is a final version that is strictly a small lithograph, slightly different from the previous versions, with no text at all and a credit line reading "Lith. & Pub. by N. Currier 2 Spruce St. NY."[189]

Based on the number of sales reported by the *Sun*, "that *The Awful Conflagration of the Steam Boat Lexington* was both a commercial and a journalistic success seems very likely," lithographic historians James Brust and Wendy Shadwell concluded.[190] After looking into the story of the lithograph, they were surprised that initially they could never find a copy of the first version. And because the next four versions they did locate were anonymous and different than any that can be definitively attributed to Nathaniel Currier, it is unclear if he did the early versions or some other artist produced them. They also note stylistic variation over the course of the printings. They point out that in the early anonymous lithograph, the *Lexington* appears stationary.

There is an attempt to show movement in the waves but they more nearly resemble snow-capped peaks. Figures in the water appear limp and insubstantial; no movement is expressed by those jumping off. As this version was presented as a daytime scene and as it was not originally colored, the artist could indicate flames only ineffectually as white patches separated from the sky by dark smoke. It appears to be the work of a poor or immature artist who is not up to the challenge of working quickly and producing a forceful image.

They add that by contrast, the next version is dramatic:

The night scene with moon and clouds reveals the boat rushing along, a swirl of flames and smoke streaming behind it. The water is choppy; the central section realistically reflects the light while the sides are darker, a device that focuses the viewer's attention as well as being visually appealing. The people and objects in the water are well distributed and give the impression of truly being in the water. A fine image—vivid and exciting—it lives up to its title description, "awful." It is to Currier's credit that he engaged an artist with the skill to create it.[191]

Although there are color versions of the Currier lithograph, Brust and Shadwell were unable to determine when they first became available:

The item in the regular edition of the Sun *on Thursday, 23 January 1840, seems to imply that color was added only with the appearance of the revised lithograph on that date, the one clearly attributed to Nathaniel Currier. Was Currier brought into the project because his shop was capable of producing hand-colored images in large quantity? That is certainly possible, though his ability to do color would not preclude his having done the earlier version as well.*[192]

Currier sold eight-by-twelve-inch hand-colored prints for eleven months. The prints depict a dramatic image with flames engulfing the middle of the vessel in the center and smoke billowing into the upper left, offset by the moon and the night sky in the upper right to create an even more menacing scene. The water is filled with live floating people—some miraculously still sporting top hats—but not corpses. That would have been too gruesome for his audience at the time; other figures sit on cotton bales or wreckage. To the right of the steamboat is a sail, probably belonging to the sloop *Improvement* that was wrongfully blamed for ignoring the disaster.[193]

Brust and his co-author, who died in 2007, predicted that additional versions of the Currier lithograph and text page would emerge over time, and that turned out to be the case. In the fall of 2022, Brust examined photos of a hand-colored page that had been sold by an antique newspaper dealer and determined it had never been seen before by lithographic historians. Brust concluded it was probably the last of the extra edition versions printed by the *Sun*, between January 25 and 28, before it turned over the printing to Currier.

Brust has catalogued fifteen distinct *Lexington* extras either published by the *Sun* with the Currier lithograph or an earlier version by an anonymous lithographer. "And I'm sure there are more out there," Brust told the author.

Besides Currier's version, there were numerous other less captivating lithographic prints, including one by Currier's former fellow apprentice John H. Bufford. Brust and Shadwell and later Brust on his own found twelve additional lithographs in addition to Currier's versions, including three by D.W. Kellogg & Company of Hartford, Connecticut; two by Bufford in New York, one of which was issued with text similar to the *Sun*'s extras as a supplement in the city's *Morning Dispatch*; and even two created in France, by L. Turgis of Paris and Lemercier Benard.[194]

Bufford's version is more detailed and professional looking than the initial one Hewitt did for the *Sun* and Currier, but it is less dramatic and not as well known today. Daniel Wright Kellogg's print is close to Hewitt's version but also deemphasizes the drama of the fire and smoke. Turgis's fanciful one is similar in style to works of famed English artist J.M.W. Turner.[195]

But as a result of Currier's speed in preparing the image, its publication in extra editions of a daily newspaper and the dramatic scene itself, *Awful Conflagration of the Steam Boat Lexington* became the most widely distributed news illustration of its generation.

Not everyone was happy to see the shocking images in circulation. On January 20, the *Boston Atlas* wrote, "We were sorry to see…displayed at the window of a respectable bookstore a picture purporting to represent the burning of the steamer *Lexington*. One would suppose it was enough to mourn the loss of dear friends without having…one's feelings lacerated by an attempt to picture the means of their death."[196]

The *Lexington* lithograph sealed Currier's reputation, which continued to grow afterward. He took on James Merritt Ives, a skilled bookkeeper, as his partner in 1852. Before shutting down in 1907, the firm billed itself as "the Grand Central Depot for Cheap and Popular Prints." The subjects of Currier & Ives' more than 7,400 prints included maritime scenes, horse

Right: Extra edition page of the New York *Sun* featuring the famous Nathaniel Currier lithograph. Historian James Brust identified it in the fall of 2022 as probably the last version of the page printed by the newspaper before Currier began printing his own version of the image. *Author photo.*

Below: One of two lithographs of the *Lexington* disaster printed in France. *Ferdinand Perrot del., Incendie du bateau a vapeur Lexington, after 1840. Lithograph, 19 x 23 cm. Courtesy of the American Antiquarian Society.*

Left: One of John Henry Bufford's two lithographs of the *Lexington* ablaze was published on a supplement page printed by the New York *Morning Dispatch*. *Courtesy of the Old Print Shop.*

Below: Lithograph of the *Lexington* signed E. Weber. *Author photo.*

races, railroads heading to the American West, hunting and fishing, fires and firefighters and even political cartoons.[197]

Robert K. Newman, an owner of the Old Print Shop in Manhattan, noted in 2012 that "Currier & Ives was the largest print publisher in the world—ever."[198] It was Currier's lithograph of the sinking of the *Lexington* that propelled him and his firm to fame and resulted in the multitudinous images we have of nineteenth-century America.

7

THE INQUEST

Because of the enormity of the disaster, Coroner Ira B. Wheeler convened a "Jury of Inquest" in Manhattan on January 19, six days after the *Lexington* left the city for the last time. The twelve jurors—all male—heard eight days of testimony before issuing their damning and controversial findings on the evening of the ninth day. Their report lists 138 people aboard the *Lexington*, but current estimates go as high as 150.

The most riveting testimony, naturally, came from three of the four survivors, as described in chapter 4. Second Mate David Crowley was still recuperating on eastern Long Island from exposure and frostbite. But there were many other witnesses who had knowledge of the steamboat and the victims. Because of the public interest in the fire, the newspapers printed long transcripts of the testimony after each session.

At the end of January, the coroner's office published a full transcript titled *Proceedings of the Coroner in the Case of the Steamer Lexington, Lost by Fire on the Thirteenth of January, 1840*. In addition, H.H. Brown and A.H. Stillwell of Providence published *Loss of the Lexington. January 13, 1840*, a summary of "The Inquest Upon the Bodies" with some verbatim testimony and some paraphrasing culled from the newspaper transcripts. The title page of the thirty-two-page booklet includes this tongue-tying description: *Loss of the Lexington of All the Circumstances Attending the Loss of the Steamboat Lexington, in Long-Island Sound, on the Night of January 13, 1840; As elicited in the evidences of the witnesses examined before the Jury of Inquest, held in New-York immediately after the lamentable event*. The page notes that "a portion of the

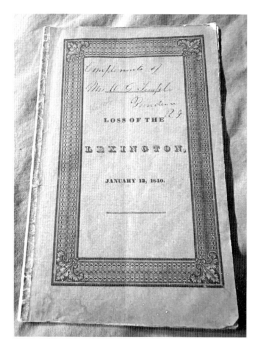 

Left: H.H. Brown and A.H. Stillwell of Providence printed this thirty-two-page pamphlet containing highlights of the testimony at the coroner's inquest following the sinking. *Right*: The title page of Brown and Stillwell's pamphlet of inquest testimony highlights. *Author photos.*

profits of this work will be appropriated to the benefit of the destitute families of those who were lost."

Before getting into the testimony, the publishers of *Loss of the Lexington* offered a flowery introduction with a prediction that turned out not to be accurate: "The 13th of January, 1840, is a day that will never be forgotten in this country—associated as it is with a calamity scarcely paralleled even in the mournful catalog of steamboat disasters."[199]

Day One

The leadoff witness was by far the most prominent: the designer and initial owner of the *Lexington*, Cornelius Vanderbilt. He told the jury he had built about two dozen steamboats. As recounted in chapter 3, he testified about the construction of the vessel launched in April 1835 and noted he had sold it in December 1838. Vanderbilt then moved on to safety issues. "I was on board of her when she was being repaired, about six weeks ago, and…she was sound.…My brother [Jacob], who was Captain, would never have gone in her if she had not been in first rate order."

Then the Commodore touched on the issue of the smokestack and carrying a cargo of cotton bales around it. He said the smoke exhaust pipe was surrounded by an empty space eight inches wide that was filled with steam to prevent the heat of the smoke pipe from igniting the outer coating and the wood casing surrounding it. "I did not consider it any more dangerous to burn coal than wood in her," he said.[200]

The next witness was Thomas E. Shaw, a "carman" or person who drives a wheeled vehicle. He testified that he had identified the body of deckhand Benjamin Laden, who was born in the Albany area, was twenty-six or twenty-seven, had no family and lived aboard the steamboat. Shaw was followed by shopkeeper William Johnson, who recognized two of the bodies in "the dead-house" as Laden and deckhand Silas Thorburn.[201]

The fourth witness was shipyard co-owner Joseph Bishop, who detailed the construction of the steamboat, as described in chapter 3. Bishop said that "about the chimney there was all the precaution against fire usual." He also described maintenance done for the Transportation Company. "We repaired her about two months ago. We mended her copper; there were some pieces of plank put in the waist," or the center of the vessel, above the waterline. "When she was taken off the dock, we considered her a strong, safe boat."[202]

The final witness on the first day was Captain Elihu S. Bunker, who in 1815 had been the first steamboat skipper to venture onto Long Island Sound. By 1840, he was working as a steamboat inspector for New York under the Safety Act of 1838, passed by Congress to try to stem the increasing number of steamboat accidents.

Bunker said he was required by law to inspect steamboat hulls twice a year and their machinery annually. He had inspected the *Lexington* on October 1: "I considered her sound in every respect; I gave her a certificate…that the boat is sound and sea-worthy."

While there had been much public speculation that the cause of the fire was switching the fuel from wood to coal, Bunker disagreed: "Wood is more dangerous than coal, from the fact that sometimes in opening a furnace an eddy from the flue will carry the light cinders among combustible materials."

Because the fire on the *Lexington* had burned through the ropes connecting the steering wheel in the wheelhouse to the iron rods running under the promenade deck back to the rudder, leaving the vessel uncontrollable, the steamboat inspector testified, "I do not consider that the law prohibits the use of ropes for steering." He noted that the vessel had an emergency tiller connected to the rudder on the aft end of the promenade deck. He added that "the intent of the law is, that rods or chains shall be used instead of ropes, for the distance running past the boilers—that is, in case of fire from the furnace, the steering apparatus may not be burnt off."

The inspector told the jury that "the manner in which she took fire is a mystery.…It is not possible, that, as coal was used, a spark from the furnace could have caught anything about the boiler."

The inspector ended the day's testimony by speaking in support of the deceased captain. "I knew Captain Child; he had a good deal of experience. I never saw anything about him that would prevent my going in a boat with him."[203]

Bunker's fellow steamboat inspector John Clark testified on the fifth day. The machinist stated, "I have worked at and made almost every kind of engine for the past thirty years." He testified about examining the *Lexington* on October 1 with Bunker. "I looked at the machinery and examined the boiler as far as it could be seen" because it was under repair and partially dismantled. "I did examine the steering apparatus," even though that was not part of his official duties. "Our certificates relate to the soundness of the boilers, engine and hull of the boat." As to whether the inspectors had ever found flaws serious enough to prohibit a steamboat from sailing, Clark said, "We have never condemned a boat or stopped its running. We have restricted boats to the use of a certain amount of steam."

Raising questions about the effectiveness of the inspections under the law in effect at the time, Clark testified, "We examined the steamer *William Young*, and found that she was not a safe and seaworthy vessel, but we gave a certificate that she was a suitable boat to run on the route."

When a juror asked, "Is cotton suitable freight to carry on board of a steamboat?" Clark replied, "Cotton is not a fit article to carry on the deck of a passenger steamboat. It is…dangerous freight."

Having been inspected on October 1, 1839, by Bunker and Clark, the *Lexington* was not due for a boiler inspection until April 1, 1840, and a hull inspection until October 1, 1840. So neither man had inspected the steamboat after the Transportation Company had made alterations a month after the last inspection. Neither inspector commented on or was questioned about those alterations during the inquest.[204]

DAY TWO

The first witness on the second day was Captain William Comstock, general agent and superintendent of the company that owned the *Lexington*, the New Jersey Steam Navigation and Transportation Company. Comstock, the principal supervisor of the company's five steamboats, had been with the company since its founding as the Boston and New York Transportation Company, being named captain of the *Fulton* in 1823 and general agent in 1837.

As described in chapter 3, Comstock said Robert Schuyler, then the company president, purchased the *Lexington* for $60,000 in 1838. The superintendent said he was not consulted on the purchase, had not examined the *Lexington* beforehand and estimated the vessel was worth about $40,000 at the time. But he added, "I thought her the fastest boat on the route."

Comstock stated that after the steamboat was purchased, the company made between $10,000 and $12,000 in improvements before putting the *Lexington* into service the previous March:

> *At the time of her purchase I made a thorough examination of every part, and took an inventory of everything on board. I found sundry defects about the engine....The smokepipe was repaired by putting in some sheets of iron. New flues were put into the boiler by Secor & Co., at an expense of $4,800....In changing the fuel from wood to coal, the grate bars were raised about 18 inches, and the furnaces contracted by filling in with brick and mortar. Under the grate were water pans always kept full....We had a blowing apparatus—what is termed a fan—made of cast and wrought iron....The fan blowers did not increase the liability for the sparks to fly out on opening the furnace doors. I considered that the adoption of coal for wood, as fuel, lessened the danger from fire, at least 50 percent. On repairing the boat, I put on the top of the boiler, a coating of zinc, fore and aft, the whole length, and think her better secured in this respect than any other boat out of New York....One foot over the zinc boiler covering was a wooden deck, over which was a sheeting of copper.*

That was not the end of the upgrades. "She was thoroughly overhauled last fall, previous to being put on the winter route." Copper plates were added to the hull and splintered wood on the keel replaced. "All the repairs were made without regard to expense. I recommended her to be put on the line for the winter, as she was a very sure boat, had a powerful engine and we could better depend upon her than some other boats on the line."

Fire was the greatest threat to a steamboat, Comstock testified. "There is necessarily on board of a steamboat a great number of fires, lights, &c." He said he had been on three boats where fire broke out, "which tended to increase my fears." He said there were at least a half-dozen stoves on the *Lexington*. The cinders removed from the furnaces were thrown into a cast-iron pipe that led overboard.

The superintendent described the two distinct sets of steering gear. The primary one consisted of iron rods running from near the stern forward to within six feet of the steering wheel and attached to it with rawhide ropes. "Chains might be substituted for the rope, but I would not trust the boat with chains to pass through Hell Gate [a stretch of turbulent water with many rocks in the East River near today's Astoria], especially in cold weather, as they would be liable to break by a sudden turn of the wheel." He added that the chain would also be apt to kink so "I recommended to the Company not to use the chains." The second steering apparatus was a tiller at the rear end of the promenade deck connected to the rudder and controlled by chains on either side of the boat. "I saw this apparatus in order before the boat left on her last trip."

Supervision of the loading of cargo was "left wholly to the Captains—though I always go on board before a boat's leaving.…No freight is ever put below deck. All the lading [cargo] is confined to the main deck, which is protected from the weather or from sparks by the promenade deck. I never saw any combustible freight stowed within three or four feet of the wood casing of the steam chimney, nor should I apprehend the least danger if it was put in direct contact therewith."

In terms of fire suppression, Comstock said the portable fire engine was located toward the bow with sixty feet of hose. "The engine and hose were new, and in perfect order." Before the last voyage, Comstock said he asked the first mate about the fire engine and was told all was in order and that it could be rigged and working in two to three minutes. But the superintendent added that water to supply the engine must be "procured from over the side by a hose thrown overboard. It would be impossible to obtain water by means of this pipe, were the boat going at the rate of even four knots [4.6 miles per hour]. The proper course to be pursued, in case a cry of fire was given, would then be to stop the engine." (That proved to be impossible when the fire broke out on the *Lexington*. And the problem was compounded by the fact that flames engulfed the end of the hose before the fire engine could be used.) Comstock said the vessel was also equipped with between two and three dozen fire buckets hanging beneath the promenade deck near the engine. "The standing order is, to have part of these buckets filled…in case of any danger."

"The *Lexington*, about four weeks ago [three weeks before the final voyage], took fire on her main deck, while lying at the wharf," Comstock continued. "Fire caught from a spark, which came probably from the kitchen-door, which fell behind a box of goods. The damage was slight."

As for the fatal blaze, Comstock said, "I cannot imagine whether it might have been taken from a fireman's lamp, or from a backdraft from the furnace, or from some other cause."

The steamboat was equipped with three boats: two twenty-foot-long "quarter-boats" mounted on either side toward the stern and a "life-boat" about twenty-four feet long rated to hold sixty persons, although Comstock thought it could not accommodate more than forty. The lifeboat was stored on the starboard, or right, side of the promenade deck almost alongside the wheelhouse. (All three were launched but lost.)

As to the qualifications of the captain, who had been with the Transportation Company for four years, Comstock said, "I have known Captain Childs for twenty years.…He commanded a vessel of mine for five years prior to his running a steamboat." Comstock said he had recommended to the board of directors that they hire Child. "I have been [on] many passages with him. I considered him as good a pilot of the Sound as any other."

The superintendent said he learned of the disaster at two o'clock on Wednesday afternoon when a steamboat from Norwalk, Connecticut, arrived in the city with the news. "The Directors of the company were immediately called together. The course recommended was to employ a steamer and proceed in pursuit of the wreck, and save all the lives and property possible. This course was immediately adopted. I employed the steamer *Statesman*, Captain Peck." It departed Thursday morning at eight o'clock under the supervision of his nephew Joseph J. Comstock. "The *Statesman* returned about 9 o'clock on Saturday morning. She had on board the life-boat, five of the bodies, and several trunks and packages of goods, from the wreck of the *Lexington*."

Comstock said the company had fire insurance of about $10,000 for each of its five steamboats but no marine casualty insurance. "We think that the risk is so little, considering the good quality of the boats and the skill of the Masters, that we had rather run our own risks."[205]

The day after he testified, Comstock sent a letter to the coroner to correct misinformation he had given in his testimony. He said the cost of

An illustration of the *Lexington* ablaze in the Brown and Stillwell pamphlet. *Author photo.*

repairs on the boilers and steam engine was more than $5,000 the previous winter; the flue in the chimney was repaired rather than replaced with a new one; the maximum amount of fire insurance on any of the company's steamboats was $20,000, not $10,000; the previous fire on the *Lexington* four weeks earlier was discovered under two boxes of goods after arrival at the wharf in New York from Stonington, and the damage claimed by the owner was $13.[206]

DAY THREE

William Comstock was followed the next morning by his nephew Joseph. He stated that he was twenty-seven and a native of Providence, where he still lived.

Comstock, captain of the *Massachusetts* for three years, said that after he learned of the disaster from a barkeeper he immediately went to the company office. After being instructed to take a steamboat to the scene of the disaster as soon as possible,

> *arrangements were made to start next morning at 8 o'clock, as no boat could be procured sooner. The steamer* Statesman, *Captain Peck, was procured....She was provided with 13 or 14 men, all told—her usual number of hands is 5 or 6. I saw that she was provided with a good boat and oars....We encountered great difficulty in getting through the ice as far as Sand's Point* [near the western end of Long Island Sound on

the southern shore], having spoken [with] every vessel between here and the Point, endeavoring to learn the position of the wreck. We then searched the shore…keeping at the same time a good look out, from the highest part of the boat, upon the water.

Comstock went ashore for the first time at Eatons Neck, on the Long Island shore forty-five miles from New York. He said the only information he could glean was that a vessel had been seen ablaze on Monday night. The *Statesman* continued east sixteen miles to the Old Field Point Lighthouse.

The first thing on landing, I saw the body of Philo Upson—it had been drawn upon the beach and was covered with cotton bagging or some sort of canvas.

I knew him from a memorandum book which was lying upon his cap, beneath his arm. Inside, the book there was nothing intelligible, but on the outside was his address in very legible characters. His countenance was very well preserved and he had on a life preserver. He was dressed in a black body coat and black pantaloons. He had a handkerchief around his body, to which was attached a four inch manilla rope. My reason for measuring the rope was, that I afterwards found a baggage crate with a rope of corresponding description. Nothing about the body indicated that it had been meddled with. We learned that the body had been picked up by the keeper of the light-house at Old Field Point, and his assistants. He told me that he found the body at daylight in the morning in the water at high water mark…on Thursday.

I left a man ashore to take charge of the body, and had it conveyed to a barn at the light-house.

The only information Comstock could gather from witnesses at the lighthouse was that they had seen the flaming steamboat about 7:30 p.m. to the west-northwest. Since night was falling, the *Statesman* crossed the Sound to Bridgeport after leaving a man on shore to make further inquiries. "Another object of my going to Bridgeport was to get news to New York, in order to relieve the anxiety existing here, and I also wished to have plenty of wood on board, though I had then enough to last for three days." From Bridgeport, he traveled by land six miles west to Southport to see *Lexington* pilot Stephen Manchester, whom he had known for ten years.

He informed me that on his first hearing the alarm of fire, he being then at the wheel on the forward extremity of the promenade deck, he opened the wheel-house door and looked out. He saw no fire nor anything to indicate fire. [Manchester testified he saw flames and smoke as soon as he stepped out of the wheelhouse.] *He stepped out some 12 or 16 feet to a small scuttle in the deck, which looked directly down to the fire room. All that he could see was a little fire; his view was, however, almost entirely obscured by a dense smoke, He stepped immediately back to the wheel-house and hauled the boat's head for the land of Long Island; while in the act of doing this, Captain Child came also to the wheel-house and ordered him to haul the boat in for the land. He replied, "I'm doing so." The captain then laid hold of the wheel to assist him....Captain Child said nothing to him about the fire at the time, but only said, "Haul her in for the land." The captain came to him very precipitately, and seemed to be out of breath.*

Capt. M. said, that when Captain Childs came up, himself and another man had hold of the wheel, and that Captain Child taking hold with them, they carried the wheel over so hard, that they carried away something. What was carried away, he could not or did not say. By this time the fire and smoke came up from beneath the promenade deck into the wheel-house with such violence, that they were compelled to relinquish their posts. He did not say what time elapsed between the alarm of fire, and the time when they left the wheel. From his manner of speaking, I consider but little time could have elapsed. After this he saw nothing of the captain.

Manchester told Comstock that he began immediately to clear away the lifeboat, which was lashed on the port or left side of the promenade deck near the wheelhouse. Having cleared away the lashings, Manchester procured a length of rope and secured it to the bow of the lifeboat and ordered it to be attached to the steamboat to keep it clear of the thrashing paddlewheel. With the fire already burning the stern of the lifeboat, he threw his pea jacket and coat into it and pushed it overboard with assistance from men he did not know. Either the rope broke or was not tied correctly, however, because the lifeboat was drawn into the paddlewheel and pushed underwater. Comstock said that when he recovered the lifeboat, it "was scorched considerably aft."

Comstock testified that Manchester told him that he went forward to the forecastle area near the bow and saw that smoke and fire filled the space under the promenade deck. The pilot said there were twenty-five or thirty people with him, including Mr. Hoyt, Mr. Van Colt, William Nichols, a "colored" man and several of the firemen and waiters.

"He saw that the boat must inevitably burn up, and that no means could save her," Comstock related. "I think he said he advised to open the baggage crates, throw out the baggage and make a raft of the crates. This was partially done. The baggage was thrown overboard, and the crates were entirely emptied and [the contents] thrown overboard." He added that "the persons who were with him acted very coolly, and made efforts to fasten them together."

But the bobbing crates proved unmanageable "and nothing could be done with them." Manchester said nothing of any attempt to reach the emergency steering apparatus at the stern. He did say that any attempt to communicate with those farther back on the main deck or obtain fire buckets there was blocked by the fire, and the flames were spreading along the promenade deck.

"While endeavoring to lash the crates, the forecastle deck became very hot from the fire beneath, and some of the persons were employed in throwing water upon it to keep it cool. The only article they could procure with which to bail water was some specie [coin] boxes which they had opened, and thrown the specie overboard." The boxes were filled from a hand pump on the forward deck.

"Seeing that the crates were of no use, they then knocked off the bulwarks and endeavored to make of them a raft, the fire all the while driving them forward, inch by inch. In consequence, they could not make a sufficient raft to hold the persons who were there."

With "the flames then rushing from the forecastle in a column 10 feet in height. Capt. M. then left the boat, and endeavored to get on whatever came in his way." He climbed on a makeshift raft. "From this he got on a bale of cotton, on which there was already another man. Another person jumped from the boat on the bale of cotton, which knocked Mr. Manchester's first companion off. Manchester hauled this man back again, there being then three persons on the bale. Manchester said that he left the bale [he did not say what time] and got upon a piece of the [paddlewheel] guard."

Manchester told Comstock that the remains of the *Lexington* sank

about three o'clock in the morning by his watch, which he took out and looked at by the light of the moon. He had a piece of plank from the bulwark, which he used as a paddle by way of exercise. He remained upon the guard until toward noon the next day, when he was taken off by a sloop. On seeing the sloop he put his handkerchief upon the piece of plank and raising it as a signal of distress, he clasped his arms around the plank and remained. Before the sloop reached him he fell over on his face and became insensible, and so remained until after he was taken on board the sloop.

After speaking with Manchester, Comstock returned to Bridgeport and sent a report to the company. At three o'clock on Friday morning, he reboarded the *Statesman* and returned to Old Field Point. "It was at this time intensely cold, the thermometer varying from 3 to 4 degrees below zero." His group had been augmented by six volunteers from New York who had friends on the *Lexington*, and they were joined at Old Field Point by Samuel Yeaton of New York City. Comstock left six men at Old Field to look for luggage.

The previous night, the body of a child about age four had been found west of the point by William Kennedy, the man Comstock had previously left ashore by the lighthouse. At eight o'clock in the morning, the *Statesman* began heading east while "every part of the bank was carefully explored as we progressed." Comstock put men ashore along the way to make inquiries.

After traveling seven miles east, Comstock learned that three bodies had been found in one of the *Lexington* quarter boats. He sent some men to remove the bodies but learned they had been taken to a wheelwright's shop where he found them and had them sent to Old Field Point. There he "learned that 18 miles farther East a man had got ashore alive" at Fresh Pond Landing near Riverhead. The *Statesman* headed there, those on board exploring the beach the entire way. "During this distance we found numerous portions of the wreck, among which was one piece [called a nameboard] on which was the entire word *Lexington*, in letters two feet in height."

As the steamboat neared Riverhead, Comstock was forced to abandon his search of the shoreline "owing to the large quantities of drift ice, and shoal water and rocky bottom, which abounded." The search crew reached Fresh Pond Landing at four o'clock on Friday afternoon.

> *Here, in consequence of the ice on the beach, we could not get on shore. We made signals, and drew to the beach some six or eight people.…We learned that David Crowley, second mate of the* Lexington, *had come ashore at 9 o'clock on Wednesday night. He stated to these people that he had been forty-eight hours upon the bale of cotton, and had crawled several rods* [a rod is 16.5 feet] *upon the beach through the ice, and after getting ashore he walked three quarters of a mile to the nearest house. They said that his feet and legs were badly frozen. He was bare headed and in his shirt sleeves. He supposed himself to be the only one saved from the wreck. I gave instructions to leave nothing undone to render his situation as comfortable as possible, and to procure for him all medical or other aid that might be necessary. They said he was in the best of hands, and that he was in want of nothing for his comfort.*

From the Christian Watchman

LOSS OF THE LEXINGTON.

A fearful cry was heard,
It rent the evening air,
The mighty deep was stirr'd,
Up rose the anguish'd prayer,
The firmest heart grew sick and faint,
As onward roll'd the wild complaint.

The mother of her child
Was suddenly bereft,—
The sire in agony, and wild,
Pray'd for dear ones left ;
The scorching fire—the chilling waves,
Ope'd widely for the travellers' graves.

The husband, faithful—kind,
Was lost in keenest wo,
He thought of *one* behind,
Whom he had cherish'd so,
And look'd upon the fearful sight
With trembling heart, that fatal night.

The child who'd gone to rest,
Soon found a troubled bed,
Without a mother's breast
To lean its aching head,
And clasp'd its little hands to say
"Our Father," 'heat an infant pray.'

The sister's friendly heart
Thought of a brother's love,
And wept that they must part—
Me't but in worlds above,
And sighed to press his hand once more,
But soon her struggling sighs were o'er.

The little ones *there* found
A fearful place of rest,
With coral reefs around,
Beneath the ocean's breast,
The boiling sea, their early grave,—
No trembling parent's hand could save.

Sad was that happy hearth
When the dread tidings came—
The messenger of truth,—
The record of the flame,

Expectant souls were stricken sore,
And dearest earthly hopes were o'er.

The mother mourns her child—
The sire, an only son,
The maiden, in delirium wild,
Weeps her betrothed one ;—
The husband—brother—sister—friend,
In mourning will together bend.

The deep—the mighty deep
Will rest the sufferer's head—
The ocean's roar their vigils keep,
And sea-weed crown their bed,
The foaming surge their funeral pall
'Till the archangel's trump shall call.

The spring flowers soon will come
Around the new made graves,
But ah ! no flow'rets bloom
Beneath the chilling waves,
Save these blest ones to memory dear,
And nurtur'd by affection's tear.

Deep—deepest grief will seize
'Reft hearts, from that sad hour,—
Will Jesus kindly please
To lend his sovereign power,
Send healing balsam from the skies—
Some angel hand to wipe their eyes—
And let them in thy mercies share,—
For every providence prepare.

Afflictions from above
Come from a FATHER's hand—
His chastisements are love,
And just is his command ;
HE can subdue the raging sea,
Or bid the wintry tempest flee,—
His hand can quench the raging flame—
Write on the burning cloud HIS name.

JUSTITIA.

Hartford, Ct. Jan. 23, 1840.

A poem included in the Brown and Stillwell booklet. *Author photo.*

Comstock authorized the people at the landing to search for other persons or property from the *Lexington* and to secure any bodies or baggage found and provide information to the New York City newspapers.

Then "I was compelled to relinquish the expedition on account of the severity of the weather, and of the sudden accumulation of ice, which rendered farther efforts useless."

The *Statesman* returned to Old Field Point and retrieved five bodies, luggage, the lifeboat and the members of the search team. "The bodies brought up were those of Mr. Waterbury, Mr. Upson, the child, and of two men unknown, which had the appearance of being those of two of the boat hands." The lifeboat—still containing Manchester's coat and jacket—had washed up two miles west of the lighthouse.

At every place they had stopped, Comstock alerted the residents "that a reward would be given for any bodies discovered, and offering also a reward of five hundred dollars for the detection of any persons committing depredations upon the bodies or property which might come ashore from the wreck."

The *Statesman* left for New York about six o'clock on Friday evening. "In consequence of the ice we were 15 hours in reaching New York, and arrived at 9 o'clock on Saturday morning."

After describing his search-and-rescue mission, Comstock returned to the subject of the *Lexington* itself and its crew. "She was a good boat, and by many considered one of the best boats running on the Sound. I was acquainted with Captain Child, and think he was every way qualified for the duties of his office. My brother was clerk of the *Lexington*….I have been on board of the *Lexington* several times since the fuel has been changed from wood to coal; and have made one passage in her with my family."

The captain said, "We as masters of the company's boats, have general instructions to leave nothing undone, without regard to expense, to render everything as safe as possible, particularly as relates to danger from fire. The boats of the company are better fitted and provided, and better guarded against fire than any others in America."

The story of the sloop *Improvement* not coming to the aid of the *Lexington* was part of Comstock's testimony:

> *I was informed by Mr. Samuel Yeaton, mate of the ship* Helirium, *that Capt. William Tirrell, of the sloop* Improvement, *of Brookhaven, stated to him that at the time the fire broke out on board of the* Lexington, *(about half past 7 o'clock in the evening), he was sailing past in the*

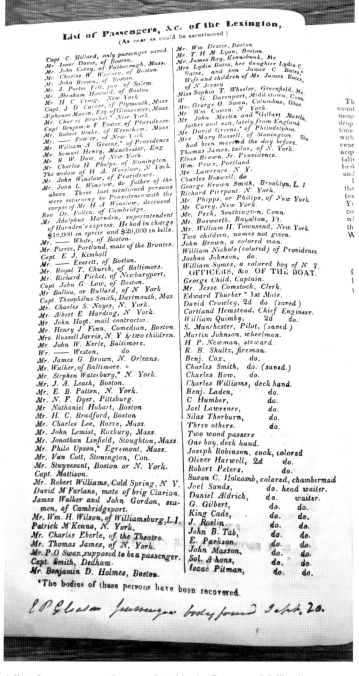

A list of passengers and crew printed in the Brown and Stillwell pamphlet. *Author photo.*

Sound on board of his sloop—he was then about six miles distant. He gave as a reason for not going to the relief of the Lexington, *that as she had life boats on board, and being near the shore, the passengers might in all probability get ashore. Another reason given by him was, that if he delayed, he should lose his tide over the bar. He could probably not have reached the wreck in less than an hour's time. He might then probably have saved many on board excepting those who were lost in the quarter boats* [when they were swamped].

This section of the Brown and Stillwell transcript is followed by a footnote that states that the crew and a passenger who had been on the *Improvement* had provided a statement to the New York *Courier* "fully exculpating Capt. Terrell from the odium which has been cast upon him on account of not repairing to the assistance of the victims lost from the *Lexington*. At the time the light [from the fire] was seen the *Improvement* was 10 or 12 miles from the *Lexington*, wind dead ahead; and the light was seen by them but a few minutes, when it disappeared."[207] (While it would have taken a long time for the sloop to tack up to the scene of the fire, that vessel likely could have arrived on the scene before the *Merchant*, which was trapped in the harbor at Southport by the ice until the following day. But there's no way of knowing if additional passengers or crew might have been saved.)

DAY FOUR

The fourth day of the inquest was taken up entirely by the testimony of the sole surviving passenger, Captain Chester Hillard, before an overflowing crowd of observers.

Before Hillard testified, coroner Ira Wheeler made a statement to the jurors paraphrased in the Brown and Stillwell pamphlet but not included in the coroner's own published transcript. Wheeler said that

among individuals, and even a portion of the city press, some dissatisfaction had been expressed in relation to the course he had pursued in the investigation, inasmuch as the witnesses as yet examined had been persons connected with or in the interest of the steamboat company. He, however, assured the jury, and wished the public to understand, that it was his fixed determination to examine minutely into all the facts and circumstances, of the case; and though the witnesses first examined were those connected with the company, the fact of their having been first called would in no wise operate as a bar to the introduction of adverse testimony; and that whatever facts might be in possession of the witnesses yet to be called, (of whom there are a large number) though tending to the blame and censure of the company, he should spare no effort to bring such facts to light, fall the odium where it might, by the evidence elicited.[208]

Hillard testified that he was born in Norwich, Connecticut, was twenty-four and had "followed the sea" for about six years. For the past eight years, his home had been in "Port Ann" (probably Fort Ann, upstate), New York, where he had moved to learn the woolen manufacturing business. After working in that trade for two years, he went to sea with Captain William Stout on the *McClellan* sailing from New Orleans.

I first went before the mast [where non-officers lived] *as a raw hand; I went five voyages before the mast, which took me in all about three years; I then went as 3d mate of the ship* Sheridan, *Captain Russell, to Liverpool, one voyage. I then went 2d mate to the ship* Mississippi, *Captain Davis, to New-Orleans and Liverpool: I then went as chief mate of the same vessel, one voyage, and on the second voyage to N. Orleans in the same ship, under Capt. Beebee. Capt. B died at New-Orleans, and I brought the ship home. I then made a voyage as master of the* Mississippi *to New-Orleans and arrived here four weeks ago next Saturday. I took passage on board the* Lexington *on just Monday week, to go to Stonington on my way to Norwich. I have no family; I have three brothers and two sisters, two half brothers and one half sister; my parents are both dead; my father was a seafaring man.*[209]

After telling the jury how he survived on a cotton bale and fireman Benjamin Cox did not, as detailed in chapter 4, Hillard added that Cox "left a wife and several [it was six] children in a deplorable situation. His wretched widow offered her last 'mite,' about five dollars for the recovery of the body of her unfortunate husband. We hope that the Company... [will] see that the body of her husband, if recovered, may be restored to her without expense to herself."[210]

DAY FIVE

The lead-off witness on the fifth day was Theodosia F. Secor, an engineer and steam-engine builder with a factory on 9th Street near the East River. Secor testified that he had repaired the boiler on the *Lexington* several times. The first repair was two years earlier when he patched several small leaks. He made similar repairs in March and November 1839. In addition, in November, "upon the engine we made some small repairs," he said, adding that the factory had given "the engine a thorough overhauling."

More importantly, several days earlier in November, Secor's workers had converted the boiler of the *Lexington* to burn coal instead of wood. "We raised the fire bars and put brick work around the furnaces. The furnace was contracted by raising the bars, which was the only contraction made. We furnished a blower for the furnace. By changing the fuel from wood to coal, the danger from fire is materially lessened. As to the coal there are no sparks; the heat in the neighborhood of the furnace is more intense from coal than wood."

Secor said of the engine manufactured at the West Point Foundry, "I consider it as perfect an engine as ever was built; I think the size and power of the engine well proportioned to the boilers and boat."

As to the cause of the fire, Secor said, "I was in the fire room frequently to witness the operation of the blower. The furnace doors were opened with the damper up as well as down. No fire or sparks came out. I have no doubt that if the damper was shut a long time the return draft would throw out fire and coals from the furnace doors."

One of the jurors asked Secor "are any of the fire-rooms of the steam-boats as safe as they ought to be?" Secor answered that they were "as safe as they can well be. The fire-room of the *Lexington* was as safe, as any of them that I know of."[211]

Secor was followed by another engineer, Richard M. Hoe. He stated that the English steamboats took "more precautionary measures against fire....I

The site of the West Point Foundry in Cold Spring is now a park. *Courtesy of Scenic Hudson.*

have always thought that our steamboats were very badly secured against fire in the fire rooms." Hoe said that in the small steamers in Europe, the fire room floor and ceiling were covered by iron.

He said European boats generally had a single steering system located at the stern. Addressing the issue of the vulnerable-to-fire rawhide ropes connecting the steering wheel to the rest of the steering mechanism, Hoe said if the correct chain was used it would "work with the same convenience as ropes, and even better, as there would be less danger of their stretching or breaking." He added, "I have seen the wire tiller ropes in use in England. They appeared to answer the purpose very well. The wire rope is a recent invention. Has been known in this country about two years."[212]

Hoe was followed by steamboat inspector John Clark, whose testimony was summarized previously in this chapter.

DAY SIX

On the sixth day, the first witness was Charles O. Handy, president of the Transportation Company. He had joined what was then called the Boston and New York Transportation Company in February 1839, shortly after it purchased the *Lexington*. The company had been a voluntary association or co-partnership until it received a charter from the New Jersey legislature at the end of February 1839 and was organized as the New Jersey Steam Navigation Company on August 1 of that year.

The company president said the $60,000 paid for the steamboat and the additional approximately $10,000 for repairs was a good investment. "I don't think that a boat like the *Lexington* could have been built for $65,000 in the condition in which she was put on the route," he said.

"It is a general regulation of the company that the boats shall be equipped and fitted in the very best manner," Handy said. Before the *Lexington* blaze, there had been only two instances of fire on the company's boats, he said. One was on the *Providence*, when a small can of oil was left on a stove in the engineer's room, caught fire and was quickly extinguished. "The only other instance that I know of a boat's taking fire was reported to have happened in the *Lexington*…three or four weeks before her destruction." He said the edge of a central hatch had caught fire from a spark from wood being burned in the furnace, before the conversion to burning coal, "which had produced slight injury" to the hatch and "partially injured a box with some goods in it as freight, that it had immediately been put out without difficulty. The bill rendered for damages to the goods was $13. I called the attention of the general agent and captain immediately to the fact, and directed every precaution taken to prevent the recurrence of a similar accident."

Handy said John Vrendenburgh, the engineer serving on the *Lexington*, had been discharged at the request of Captain Jacob Vanderbilt and replaced by Cortland Hempstead because he had experience with boilers burning coal.[213]

William Kemble, president of the West Point Foundry Association, was the next witness. He testified that his company manufactured the engine and boiler at a cost of $25,000. "The engine and boiler were made of the best material, and constructed without regard to pains or expense," he stated. "So much so, that the engine when finished, was considered equal to any ever put up in New York."[214]

The jury then recalled shipbuilder Joseph Bishop, who broke down the cost of constructing the *Lexington*.[215] Steamboat inspector Elihu S. Bunker was also recalled and reiterated his qualifications and those of fellow inspector John Clark, stating, "I think there could not be found in the United States two other inspectors" with their experience.

Bunker wanted to clarify his statements about the use of rawhide rope to connect the steering rods to the steering wheel. "I said that I did not consider that the law prohibited the use of the rope *round the wheel*. I do consider the use of the *rods* is, required by law.… The rods were first introduced by myself, some fourteen years since."

Bunker also clarified how inspections were carried out:

> We examine the boat inside and out to see how she is built.… We sometimes take the certificate of a carpenter as to the soundness of the timber.… I have taken my knife and put it into the timbers.… We always inform the officers of the boat that to give us wrong information is an indictable offence.… In examining a boiler, we go all round it, and have something to strike upon it.… I can tell from the thickness of a boiler, the exact amount of pressure it will bear.

Next up was engineer Adam Hall, who had an office in Manhattan and was formerly employed by the West Point Foundry, where he constructed the engines and boilers for the *Lexington* for Cornelius Vanderbilt. "The machinery was of the best order," he said. "The fire room was as well protected from fire as they usually are on board of our boats.… Over the boiler was a sheet of iron which did not come within four or five inches of the beams."

The engineer also discussed blowers designed to increase the intensity of the boiler fire. "I have never examined the blowing apparatus of the *Lexington*. I have frequently seen similar contrivances on board of other boats. The blower produces a much greater draft than would otherwise exist. The effect is, that sometimes a great deal of fire is blown out on opening the furnace doors. I have often seen on opening the doors, not only flame, but small particles of coal, which were thrown a considerable distance."

Hall said of *Lexington* engineer Cortland Hempstead, "I was acquainted with Mr. Hempstead. Mr. Hempstead, I considered a very capable man."[216]

Day Seven

The seventh day began with *Lexington* pilot Stephen Manchester. "I follow the water for a livelihood, and have done so for about twenty years, as master, mate and pilot," he stated. "I have been pilot of a steamboat for five years… Three years past have been pilot of the *Lexington*."

The Providence native, who had been hired by the Transportation Company the previous March, said, "I considered the *Lexington* as good as any on the line, and as good as any other as far as I know." Manchester said he was not aware of an earlier fire on the *Lexington* until it was mentioned by previous witnesses.

He described his responsibilities for the jury: "My sole business is when the boat is ready to start, to go into the wheel house and there remain until she arrives at her place of destination.…I did notice the manner in which the cotton on board was stored; it was done in about the usual manner.…The freight was so stowed as to admit of a free passage fore and aft.…I never knew it otherwise."

After providing that background, the pilot recounted his harrowing experience on the final voyage as presented in chapter 4.

Manchester told the jurors, "I have known Captain Child some ten or fifteen years. We were packet [regularly scheduled vessels] masters together for several years.…He was a very steady, smart and capable man for the business in which he has been engaged."

As to the cause of the disaster, Manchester testified, "In my opinion, the fire originated from the heat of the smoke pipe, which was communicated to the wood work. I have frequently seen the smoke pipe red-hot, and saw it so on the last night.…The cotton was piled within perhaps a foot of the steam chimney—it might have been two feet. The flame which I first saw appeared to be that created by the burning of wood and not of coal."

Manchester discussed the steering gear, saying, "I never saw a boat steered wholly with rods and chains." He added that substituting chains for the rawhide ropes would be a mistake "as in cold weather the chains would be more likely to break. I think the ropes used on board of the *Lexington* were as safe as any chains that could be rigged. I don't think that had chains been used on board of the *Lexington* that I should have been more likely to have reached the shore with her." The pilot concluded by saying, "I never had any apprehension of the *Lexington*'s taking fire, nor did I consider her any more likely to take fire than any other boat."[217]

The pilot was followed by Captain Curtis Peck, owner of the steamboat *Fairfield*. "I have been concerned in steamboats for twenty years," he informed the jury. He said in 1823 he had rigged a steamboat with iron steering rods connecting to rope at each end as in the *Lexington*. But "in consequence of the complaints from passengers of the noise made by rods, I abandoned their use and resumed that of ropes altogether."

Peck said that the *Fairfield* was steered by ropes with a backup tiller fitted with chains at the stern in case of fire nearer the bow. "I consider a boat steered by ropes safer than if rigged with chains. The rope is more pliable than the chain." He said he experimented with "steering altogether with rods and chains but the chain several times parted, and were inconvenient to steer with, and in consequence I had them taken out."

As to the coal burned by the *Lexington*, "I think that coal can be used as fuel with as much safety as wood." But he added, "I have never seen a boiler that I thought was properly adapted to the use of coal as a fuel, and have always used wood myself in preference."[218]

Day Eight

The first witness on the eighth and final day of testimony was John Vrendenburgh of Manhattan, who said he had been a steamboat fireman or engineer for more than eight years. He had worked on the *Lexington*, starting as assistant engineer in the fall of 1837 and then served as engineer after a few months until he was fired the previous November by Jacob Vanderbilt, who told him it was because he "thought I had not control enough over the men."

"She had a perfect engine, and her boiler was a good one," Vrendenburgh testified. "We had it repaired last winter; we put on a new shell and chimney legs…and put a new course of boiler iron on the bottom of the smoke pipe."

"Have never known the *Lexington* to be on fire while I was on board of her," the engineer continued. "I have used coal, but never used a blower—have seen a blower used with wood on board the *North America*, and when the furnace doors was opened, the flame would come out four or five feet, and would knock a man over."

The next witness was Frederick Hempstead of Brooklyn, a steamboat engineer for seven or eight years and brother of *Lexington* engineer Cortland Hempstead. He testified that he had served as engineer aboard the ill-fated steamboat once—filling in for his sick brother on the trip before the final voyage. And he described the *Lexington* as a serious fire hazard.

Hempstead said he had worked on several other steamboats, including a stint as engineer of the *David Brown*, which ran between New York and Charleston. "We burnt coal on board of that boat with a natural draft; we had no blowers," Hempstead said. He added that he considered blowers dangerous unless the boilers were surrounded by sufficient sheet iron.

Hempstead said that while he was serving on the *Lexington*, "I was afraid of fire, because my brother told me that the boat had been on fire the trip before; he told me to look out for fire along side of the boilers, and said I should be troubled with the blowers." There were two of them, and his brother had ordered a new pulley installed before the last trip to increase their revolutions and airflow.

> *When I was in her we had a good deal of difficulty with the blowers, and my brother told me they were also troublesome to him, and had been ever since they had used them. The wood was stowed along side the boiler, and was on fire several times during the trip I was in her. When the blowers were in full operation, the coals in small pieces would come out of the furnace doors, if they were open, and that was what set the wood on fire. I have heard my brother say that he considered her a dangerous boat, and cautioned me....I consider the more revolutions the blowers make the more danger there is of fire.*

Hempstead said his brother had told him that part of a brick wall in the engine room had collapsed several times because of the force of the air emitted by the blowers. "I did not sleep any all night because of my brother's caution," he continued. When the furnaces ignited wood stored near them, "there was no difficulty in extinguishing the fire; there was a tank in front of the boiler which would hold five or six pails of water, which was placed there for that purpose."

Hempstead said he "should consider the boiler on board the *Lexington* was as safe as any other, after her alterations for burning coal, with the exception of the blower." The engineer said he had seen flames five or six feet high coming out of the top of the smokestack and "seen the smoke pipe red-hot to within about two feet of the promenade deck. The chimney was red hot most of the time on the trip I was in her."

The witness concluded by saying that "when I went on board there was a joiner [carpenter] at work on board; I asked my brother what he was doing there; and my brother said the boat had been on fire and he was repairing the damage; he was repairing the casing of the steam chimney on the larboard [port or left] side down on to the boiler hatch."[219]

Hempstead was followed by one of the four survivors, fireman Charles B. Smith of Norwich, Connecticut, whose account of the fire and its aftermath was given in chapter 4. Smith described another fire for the jury: "Have been in the *Lexington* ever since she commenced burning coal; have known her to be on fire on the 2d January, on the main deck, along side the boiler; it originated from some sparks which flew up and caught the deck; it did not burn so much as to make a blaze on deck. It burnt a corner of a box which was there, but did not damage the goods which were in it. Never knew her on fire at any other time."

According to the fireman, "when the door of the furnace is opened, the sparks from the coal do not come out, unless the damper is down, which we always keep open and fastened open."

Smith said he was aboard the *Lexington* on the trip when Frederick Hempstead served as engineer, and he contradicted Hempstead's testimony:

> [Neither] *the boat nor the wood on board was on fire during that trip, to my knowledge....We did not have the blower on, because it was broke; saw no bricks blown down at any time.....Never saw the* [wood] *casing of the steam chimney on fire; should think I should have heard of it if there had been a fire on board. Never heard of any cotton being on fire either on the wharf alongside the boat or on board the boat. Have seen the chimney red hot, have seen a blue flame come out of the top of the chimney, probably as much as six feet. Have been a fireman 4 years in different boats, and in boats where coal has been used; don't consider a boat in any more danger with a blower than without one.*[220]

John Ryno, a cartman who lived in Greenwich Village, followed Smith to the witness stand. He said he worked at Pier No. 1 on the North (Hudson) River and offered testimony about the flammability of cotton bales. "The last time the *Lexington* went out I saw a bale of cotton on fire on the dock.…There was one corner of it on fire; it lay by itself.…Saw the hands from on board the *Lexington* pouring water on it; did not see them throw but one pail on it."[221]

The final witness was ship's carpenter William Sydney Thompson. He said about three trips before the final voyage, he repaired a burn hole "about as big as my hat" on the main deck near the boiler hatch.[222]

Day Nine

Coroner Ira B. Wheeler briefly addressed the jury on the ninth and final day of the inquest:

> *Gentlemen…the investigation has arrived at that stage when it becomes your peculiar province to consider and determine on it. It would be preposterous in me to attempt directing the minds of this Jury as to the result which they are to arrive at; for each and all of them are as capable of understanding the testimony as I am. I shall therefore use no argument, or in any way attempt to lead you, knowing that you are fully competent to make up your own minds as to what, under all the circumstances of the case, should be your verdict. I however consider it my duty to remark, that my mind remains at this moment as undecided as it was before the investigation commenced, and to me the question remains involved in as much mystery as ever. Nor can I, from all the testimony which has been adduced, come to any conclusion, or be satisfied as to the origin or cause of the fire. You, gentlemen, however, may be more competent to arrive at some conclusion on the subject. But in doing so, allow me to impress upon your minds the necessity of exercising due deliberation, great care, and extreme caution. For never perhaps, did there go forth to this community, a Coroner's inquest the consequences of which were likely to affect so many public and private interests. The words of this inquest will reach the bosoms of those whose relatives have perished by this melancholy calamity, and may dispose them to resignation, or aggravate their grief, according as your verdict tells them that it was owing to unavoidable accident, or to the negligence of those in whose hands they entrusted their lives. Your verdict may also, in a pecuniary point of view, affect materially, not only the interests of the Company most immediately concerned in it, but also of several others; and hence, gentlemen, the necessity of great caution in determining on your verdict.*[223]

Wheeler then instructed the jurors that "you may either give a verdict simply saying what you think was the probable cause of the deaths of the persons on whom you are holding this inquest, or you may, in addition to such a verdict, state your opinion as to the outfit of the boat and the manner in which she was navigated. You have also a right to express your opinion as to whether the boat was fitted out according to law."[224]

When the jurors indicated they could not come to a unanimous conclusion, Wheeler explained that they were acting like a grand jury and a unanimous decision was not required, just a majority. And by the end of that day, a majority opinion had been reached.[225]

The Verdict

The verdict, announced at six o'clock, was "that the deceased, Stephen Waterbury, Philo Upson, Silas Thorburn, Benjamin Lader and Jacob C. Bates, came to their death in consequence of the burning of the steamboat *Lexington*, in Long Island Sound on the 13th instant."[226]

In addition to the simple one-sentence verdict on the cause of death of the victims whose bodies had been recovered and brought to New York, the jurors added a lengthy "presentment" dealing with the cause and responsibility for the disaster. The findings:

> *The inquest* [jurors] *are of opinion that the fire was communicated to the promenade deck by the intense heat of the smoke pipe, or from sparks from the space between the smoke pipe and steam chimney, as the fire was first seen near the casing of the steam chimney, on the promenade deck.*

This was a surprising conclusion that conflicted with the testimony of the series of experts who talked about the smoke pipe being safely insulated by the steam-filled space between the pipe and the outer edge of the chimney and the enclosing wood casing. And those experts had no explanation for the cause of the fire. These points were raised by the company and others who commented in the newspapers after the inquest.

> *That the* Lexington *was a first rate boat, with an excellent steam engine, and a boiler suitable for burning wood, but not coal, with the blowers attached.*

This opinion was shared by some of the witnesses but not by most of the experts who testified.

> *Furthermore, it is our opinion, that had the buckets been manned at the commencement of the fire, it would have been immediately extinguished.*

The jury ignored the testimony that some buckets were being used as soon as the fire was discovered and that most of the buckets were suspended above the engine in the area that was quickly overrun by the fire and so the officers and crew initially focused, unsuccessfully, on getting the steam fire pump running and then launching the boats.

> *That inasmuch as the engine could not be stopped, from the rapid progress of the fire, with presence of mind of the officers and a strict discipline of the crew, the boats could have been launched, and a large portion of the passengers, and crew, if not the whole, might have been saved.*

This was an odd and wildly speculative conclusion. With the engine still running and the *Lexington* traveling at thirteen miles per hour, it was almost impossible to safely launch the three boats. And the rapidly advancing fire did not leave time to wait for the vessel to stop before launching the boats, which probably could have not accommodated up to 150 people in any case. And passenger Hillard supported the testimony of the 3 surviving employees that the officers and crew had acted properly without any sign of panic.

> *That the present inspectors of steamboats, either from ignorance or neglect, have suffered the steamboat* Lexington *to navigate the Sound at the imminent risk of the lives and property of the passengers, giving a certificate stating a full compliance with the laws of the United States, while in our opinion such was not the case.*

This was another baffling conclusion, considering the extensive testimony that the vessel met or exceeded all federal standards. Only Frederick Hempstead, who sailed only once, had said the steamboat was in poor shape; a host of other experts testified that the *Lexington* was in first-rate condition.

> *The system, as adopted on board of the* Lexington, *of using blowers on board of boats, is dangerous, which has been proved to this jury by competent witnesses.*

While a few witnesses testified that the use of blowers increased the fire risk, this jury conclusion ignored the testimony of most of the engineers and others who said using blowers properly did not increase the danger of fire.

The conduct of the officers of the steamboat Lexington *on the night of the 13th of January, when said steamboat was on fire,* deserves the severest censure of this community. [emphasis added]

The presentment singled out the captain and pilot. Surviving crew members Crowley and Smith and passenger Hillard offered no testimony critical of the actions of Child and Manchester. Manchester was credited with getting a group of passengers and crew off the bow alive. Nonetheless, the jury wrote that "from the facts proved before this jury, that the Captain and Pilot, in the greatest hour of danger, left the steamboat to her own guidance, and sought their own safety, regardless of the fate of the passengers." This was an odd comment considering the captain died while trying to launch a lifeboat with crew and passengers and the pilot went over the side with a group on the bow after the boat they had launched became separated from the *Lexington.*

The jurors based their criticism on the fact that neither the captain nor pilot made their way to the stern to try to operate the emergency steering apparatus in an attempt to beach the steamboat at Eatons Neck. "Instead of the Captain or Pilot retreating to the tiller, aft, when driven from the wheel-house, forward, and the ropes there being burned off, there being at that time a communication to the same tiller, there appeared to be no other thought but self-preservation." While the jurors were convinced Child and Manchester could have reached the stern, traveling the length of a vessel that was ablaze amidships would likely have been difficult, if not impossible.

The odious practice of carrying cotton, in any quantities, on board of passenger boats, in a manner in which it shall be liable to take fire, from sparks or heat, from any smoke pipe, or other means, deserves public censure.

This finding echoes the testimony of steamboat inspector John Clark. But after the inquest, others would point out that cotton bales were not highly flammable in their compacted form and that they did not catch on fire until the blaze was well advanced.

The majority opinion dated January 31 was signed by a dozen of the jurors. But two, foreman Benjamin Vincent and Joseph E. Mount, dissented from the condemnation of Manchester. They said they "fully exonerate and exculpate, Capt. Stephen Manchester from any blame or censure after the breaking out of the fire on board."[227]

The Reaction

Unsurprisingly, the verdict generated a great deal of comment in the newspapers, at public meetings and from church pulpits, much of it critical of the steamboat company and its employees. The mood of the crowds at the meetings echoed the inquest jury findings. The New York *Morning Herald* reported on February 5 that at a public meeting in Boston, "the owners and directors of the *Lexington* were denounced in severe terms for their murderous conduct, and all travellers are recommended to avoid their boats. This is right and proper; we echo the sentiment and add a strong appeal to its enforcement."

But there were also a lot of letters from people from maritime backgrounds defending the company and saying the fire was an accident that defied all proper precautions taken to make the *Lexington* safe. Interestingly, the official publication of the proceedings by the coroner's office included many of these letters that had been published in the newspapers that were highly critical of the jury findings. Wheeler may have decided to do this after having already said the testimony had not answered the question of the cause of the fire for him.

Some writers accused the jury of having a bias against the company and officers on the *Lexington* and ignoring the preponderance of evidence in their favor. "It soon became apparent to the numerous spectators, who crowded around the Jury on the first two or three days of the Inquisition, that all the evidence sought for by the most active members of the Jury, was only to be of that nature to criminate either the owners, officers or inspectors of steamboats," argued a newspaper letter writer who identified himself only as VINDEX and whose highly detailed analysis filled sixteen pages of the published proceedings.

VINDEX disagreed with the jury finding that "the fire was communicated to the promenade deck by the intense heat of the smoke pipe, or from sparks from the space between the smoke pipe and steam chamber, as the fire was first seen near the casing of the steam chimney, above the promenade deck." He pointed out that "none of them [the three survivors who testified] first discovered the fire. All were informed by others." So there was no reliable evidence about the origin and spread of the fire, he wrote. "The most probable conjecture which may be drawn from the laws of nature is, that the fire originated below the promenade deck, and as the flame mounted upwards in its natural course, it communicated to the casing and so upwards to the promenade deck."

As to the second conclusion that the *Lexington* was not suited to burn coal using blowers, VINDEX wrote, "We have the opinion of all the witnesses in favor of the safety of the blower, except Mr. Hall and Mr. Hempstead, and Mr. Hall only speaks of danger in opening the doors when the blast [blower] is on," and the blast of air from the blower could be turned off as necessary. "Mr. Hempstead...never went in the *Lexington* but once, nor in any other boat that used blowers, consequently he was ignorant of their use....His opinions are contradicted by the fireman, Smith, who had actual experience of the blowers, by the testimony of the other witnesses, and by common sense."

VINDEX commented on the third conclusion, that had the fire buckets been used properly at the beginning of the fire it would have been immediately extinguished and had the officers and crew maintained strict discipline they could have safely launched the three boats and saved most if not everyone on board even if the engine could not be shut down because the fire prevented access.

> *This is undoubtedly true, provided the passengers, more numerous than the crew, likewise retained their presence of mind and kept so cool as to not interfere with the officers, and also have been disposed to assist the crew with the engine and buckets; and provided further, that the waiters and all the officers and crew were on deck at the commencement of the fire, instead of one half being below at rest....Captain Childs appears to have done all that could have been done.*

As for the steamboat inspectors being ignorant or neglectful, VINDEX pointed out that "Captain Bunker is well known, having commanded a steamboat since 1811," and had managed the construction of five steamboats. "His colleague, John Clark...superintended the building of several steamboats and steam engines for others, and was frequently consulted by the owners and builders of steamboats....So much for the ignorance of these two inspectors." As for the possibility of negligence, the writer detailed how the inspectors "had performed their duty" as specified by federal law.

About the blowers, VINDEX wrote that "as far as the proof goes, it appears that blowers are safe, if care is used to keep the damper open, and the blast shut off, when the doors are opened."

VINDEX took issue with officers deserving censure: "There is no direct evidence to show, that he [Captain Child] neglected any part of his duty.... He knew that the boat was unmanageable, on account of burning of the tiller-ropes, that the flames were spreading rapidly aft, and that the engine could not be stopped, and that if the boats were not lowered even while the engine was underway, the passengers must inevitably be destroyed by fire." VINDEX said the accusation would "inflict a wound into the bosoms of his bereaved relatives and friends." As for Manchester, VINDEX noted that the pilot thought if the emergency tiller could be used, there would be sufficient crew at the stern to use it, as he had testified: "I thought my services were more needed forward. I think that in consequence of the smoke that fell aft, a man could not have remained at the tiller until the time when the engine stopped." VINDEX noted that even if someone had been able to use the emergency tiller, the engine stopped long before the vessel would have reached shore, and if Manchester had gone to the stern, it would have prevented his efforts to launch the boat near the pilothouse. "He did not desert his duty.…He appears to have been cool and industrious for more than four hours."

And regarding the final conclusion that carrying cotton on passenger boats "deserves the public censure," VINDEX pointed out that "the jury have not found that the *Lexington* carried cotton in this dangerous manner."

Overall, VINDEX concluded, "We think we have shown from the evidence, that these conclusions can neither be supported by testimony, nor can many of them be sustained upon sound scientific principles." He suggested that the jury members "were guided more by their own knowledge and experience, than by the evidence of the witnesses." The writer pointed out that the jury members were a doctor, a dentist, an agent, a grate setter, a merchant, a tailor, a shoemaker, a printing press manufacturer, two constables and two clerks. "We are not ourselves aware that any of them are acquainted with steamboats or their machinery.…For ourselves…the cause of the fire is still involved in mystery and obscurity."[228]

More criticism came from a "Naval Officer of rank" who signed his letter "Communicated." "I have read all the testimony taken before the Coroner…and it seems to have been as purely an accident, against all human precaution, as ever took place," he wrote. "I have not yet discovered that any thing on the part of the proprietors was left undone, which could possibly ensure the safety of travellers. Had it not been for the alarm and confusion of the passengers, the fire would no doubt have been soon got under [control]. If they had been bent on self-destruction, they could not have more directly accomplished it, than to lower the quarter boats bow foremost while the Steamer was at full speed, and to heave the Life-boat over in front of the [paddle]wheels." He called the focus on the ropes connecting the iron steering rods to the steering wheel "absurd. Of what consequence is it of what the wheel ropes are made of *at the wheel*, when the same heat that would burn them, would also destroy the helmsman. Therefore, unless *iron men* can be found, the material of the ropes is not so important."[229]

A letter signed as "Truth, But Not Fiction" stated, "There has been a searching examination before the Coroner, and what has been elicited therefrom to implicate the company? I certainly perceive nothing myself. The boat was proven to be a very good one, and well found in every respect."[230]

The coroner's published report also included a letter by Captain William Comstock, the superintendent of the steamboat company, that was published in the *National Intelligencer* and dated January 27, four days before the end of the inquest.

> *No person living regrets the loss of the* Lexington *and the lives on board, more than myself. I am aware of the attacks on the directors and agents of the company. Thank God, I have nothing to reproach myself with in regard to the awful and unexpected calamity. The* Lexington, *in the month of November, was put in the very best possible order for the winter service; she was completely overhauled, from the keel to the deck—including the engine and boiler. The work was done without any regard to expense. She was furnished with three good boats, (one a life boat), with fire engine and hose…also two or three dozen fire buckets. She was also furnished with two separate and distinct steering gear.…Will any person presume to say that the pilot could remain one minute at his post after he was attacked by fire and smoke?—No: the boat, in five minutes after taking fire, was in complete flame fore and aft.* This fact I attribute to not stopping the engine immediately after the alarm was given.[231] [emphasis added]

The coroner's published report concludes with an eight-page statement of "Remarks" from the Transportation Company. "If this boat was defective in her equipment—if any precautions which enlightened judgment, and experience of this country, suggested were not put in requisition for the protection of the lives of her passengers, and the security of property, the Company have yet to be apprised of it." The company said it fully and willingly participated in the inquest, "no Counsel being present," and the "officers and agents waited not for Subpoenas to appear." This was followed by a not-so-subtle swipe at the inquest jury when the statement said the company would not question the "contradictions, nor to the want of unanimity among the jury—neither will they remark upon the qualifications of this Jury for this important task assigned to them—but will proceed to a plain narrative of what they know to be true."

The company said in its four years of running boats on Long Island Sound, "no expense has been spared by the proprietors…to render them… safe depositories of life and property." The company said it had spent $500,000 to build and equip the best boats on the Sound and had yet to see a profit, despite being accused of being a "grasping monopoly."

In the year that the *Lexington* had been owned by the company, "the repairs which were put upon her hull, boiler and machinery, deemed thorough on examination by competent persons, were made at a great expense, and the work was done by experienced and well-qualified mechanics and engineers— the object being to render her perfectly competent and safe to encounter the winter navigation of the Sound."

"Every precaution was enjoined to give all possible security to the furnaces and boiler—nor has it been proved that they were the cause of danger." The company pointed out that blowers had been used for years and were installed on at least six other steamboats traveling the same waterways. "Ordinary attention on the part of the engineer effectually remove[s] all danger of explosion."

The company pointed out that the chief engineer of the *Lexington* had never raised any concerns about burning coal with blowers. It noted the double systems of steering gear and said the attachment of the steering rods to the steering wheel with rawhide ropes was immaterial because Manchester had been driven out of the pilothouse by flames shortly after the ropes parted. The company noted that "the *Lexington* had a good portable fire engine on board (new but very recently) placed on the main deck, and convenient for use…and about forty-five buckets…and that the crew had been accustomed to the use of the engine." As required by federal law, the vessel carried three boats, including a patent lifeboat.

The company also noted cotton had been carried by "every freight and passenger steamer for years past in these and other waters.…As usually compacted into bales, cotton cannot be considered as a dangerous freight. It will not blaze unless separated from the mass.…It is further alleged that the stowage of the cotton was the proximate cause of the fire," but the company wrote that no testimony had supported that assertion.

No freight was stowed on the Promenade Deck; and the Steam Chimney of the Lexington, *surrounded by a wooden casing, extended from twelve to fourteen inches above this deck. This chimney was eight or nine inches* outside *the smoke pipe, which it encircled, and was filled, when the engine was in motion, always with steam—and was again surrounded with a wooden casing three or four inches apart from it. To ignite this casing, even if the smoke pipe were red-hot, its heat must be communicated through the mass of steam, again through the iron which formed the steam chimney, and again through the atmospheric air separating it from the casing....It does not appear that the fire originated between decks, nor that it commenced with the cotton. The cause that did produce its origin has not been discovered. One thing is certain, that whatever may have been its cause, all the means for its extinction which care and prudence could suggest, had been provided and were in the boat; nor is the allegation true that she had been on fire several times before.*

The company said there had only been one fire before the last voyage and that one was "shown to have been of trivial character."

As to the finding that the captain and officers had been negligent of their duty, "the good character of the late Captain Child, in the opinion of those who had longest known him, is incorporated with the testimony....No one probably among all who perished in that awful night, had a deeper stake for the preservation of life than himself, having a wife and several children depending on him for protection and support."

In conclusion, the company wrote, that since its inception it had "been subjected to a keen and violent opposition—inflamed and assisted by rival interests, and stimulated by...legislative encouragement....Unmoved by these assaults...it has been their aim to run no steamers but such were safe, strong, and well-equipped, and to employ no agents or officers but such as were deemed well-qualified for their post."

The *Lexington* "was purchased after a thorough examination into her strength, machinery, and other qualities. In these particulars she certainly improved rather than deteriorated in the hands of the Company; and they have only deeply to lament that with the best intentions and with un-remitted exertions to avert it, on their part, her end should have been so disastrous and tragical."[232]

Despite the criticisms of the verdict by the company and other maritime experts, the inquest firmly placed the fault for the disaster on the New Jersey Steam Navigation Company and crew in the already excited public imagination. Newspapers and their readers in the following weeks demanded that the officers of the steamboat and company be indicted for murder.

The *Morning Herald* made that argument on February 7 in an editorial rife with misinformation:

> *What will all the tedious investigation into the murderous conduct of the Directors of the* Lexington *amount to, unless the United States Attorney does his duty? Does he not mean to prepare a bill of indictment against the directors! Does he not mean to procure the instant dismissal of the ignorant and incompetent inspectors? We entreat the community not to lose sight of this important point. Justice must be satisfied. Over one hundred and twenty of our fellow beings have been murdered by the conduct of the managers of that boat, and they must be made to suffer.… The simple facts of the case are narrowed down to a very small compass: there were 100 people on board, and the three boats would hold only 70 at the most; so that one half must have perished any way; the boat was murderously loaded down with cotton close to the red-hot smoke pipe; the blower blew down the brick wall, and blew the flames and burning embers all about the boat; the boat was on fire repeatedly, and yet no extra precaution was taken to protect human life; the cotton was on fire before she started the last trip; and she had tiller ropes, round the wheel, which burnt off, instead of chains. With all these glaring facts staring us in the face, we repeat that all now living connected with the management of that boat, ought to be indicted for murder.*

Despite newspapers like the *Herald* fanning the hysteria, there would be no criminal prosecution.

There also would be no lawsuits filed against the company by the families of those who had died. In 1840, any grounds for litigation for personal injury died with the victim because common law in the United States did not recognize a cause of action for wrongful death. It was not until seven years later that New York became the first state to pass a statute allowing a person's estate to file a lawsuit for wrongful death.[233]

The inquest did produce some immediate results, however.

On February 13, the *Herald of the Times* reprinted an item from the *Providence Journal* that said, "The Transportation Company are building life boats for all their steamboats [as opposed to one lifeboat and two simple open quarter boats on the *Lexington*]. They are to be of the most perfect construction, with all the late improvements, and capable of sustaining great weight." The newspaper then added news of another important development: "We also learn that the proprietors of the boats of this company, have determined to carry no more cotton for freight."

The *Long-Islander* in Huntington commented on the cotton decision in its February 21 issue: "This is a judicious and humane determination, and it is a pity that they had not adopted the measure before the awful calamity of the *Lexington*."

Long after the *Lexington* inquest, newspapers and the public continued to urge Congress to strengthen steamboat safety regulations. But it would be twelve years after the sinking before the lawmakers took action, as detailed in chapter 10.

But with the blame for the fire and sinking established, whether fairly or not, by the inquest jury, the stage was set for litigation.

8

THE LITIGATION

There would be no criminal prosecution or civil litigation against the New Jersey Steam Navigation Company or its officers and employees for negligence. But, not surprisingly, the loss of the *Lexington* prompted lawsuits from those who suffered financial setbacks from lost cargo or possessions.

Some cases took an unusually long time to be filed or heard after the 1840 sinking, possibly because there had been unsuccessful settlement negotiations. Some cases were over relatively small losses. On July 12, 1843, the *Brooklyn Evening Star* noted on page 2 that "the courts throughout several States of the Union are uniformly deciding that common carriers are liable for the goods entrusted to them for transit. The case of the *Lexington* has given rise to some litigation in the [state] Supreme Court at New Haven on the subject." The newspaper appended a story from the *New Haven Herald* about one of the minor cases, that of Warner E. Hale, who sued the New Jersey Steam Navigation Company for the value of two carriages that went down with the vessel. The court ruled against the company, saying that the contract was covered by the laws of the State of New York and "that persons who undertake generally to transport goods for hire…and deliver them at places appointed, are deemed common carriers, whether by sea or land, through the sound or on rivers, whether in ships or in steamboats; and that common carriers are liable for goods received to transport and deliver." The carrier was held responsible unless the cargo was "not delivered except the loss arise from the act of God or the public enemies." The court also found that "the restrictions of their liability which the defendants claimed, by virtue of their notices and bill of lading, that by the laws of the State of New York, they would not…restrict their liability as common carriers." The steamboat company requested a new trial, but the judge refused. Hale had sought $500 and was awarded $450, but the navigation company planned to appeal, according to the August 10, 1842 issue of the *Journal of Commerce* in New York.

The most significant case went all the way to the U.S. Supreme Court, dragging on until almost eight years after the sinking. The litigation, of great interest to transportation companies and their clients, was filed by the Merchants' Bank in Boston, which had shipped $25,000 in gold and silver coins on the voyage. These were the coins that the survivors testified in the inquest had been thrown overboard so the casks could be used to throw water on the fire.

The bank sued on February 10, 1842, in the District Court of the United States for the District of Rhode Island. The "libel," as the suit was called, charged that the loss of the *Lexington* and the coins resulted from "the improper stowage of the gold and silver coin, the imperfect and insufficient engine, furnace, machinery, furniture, rigging, and equipments of the boat, and her careless, improper, and negligent management and conduct by the officers, servants, and agents of the respondents; and by reason thereof claims damages to the amount of twenty-five thousand dollars."

The "libellants," or plaintiff, offered evidence to prove that the furnaces were unsafe and insufficient; that there was no proper casing for the steam chimney, nor any safe lining of the deck where the chimney passed through it; that dry pine wood was habitually kept in an exposed position; that there was improper stowage of the flammable cotton cargo; that the boat lacked proper tiller chains or ropes; that the fire buckets were not properly prepared and fitted with heaving-lines; that the fire engine was kept in one part of the boat while the hose was kept in another where it was inaccessible when the fire broke out; and that the vessel had caught fire in its preceding voyage and no measures had been taken to prevent a recurrence.

The respondents, the transportation company, offered evidence that the hull, engine, boiler and general equipment were good; that the most experienced men had been employed without regard to expense in putting the vessel into proper order; that it had a captain, pilot and crew "equal to all ordinary occasions"; and that the company was not liable if they did not prove fit for emergencies. It argued that the boat was well-equipped with tool chests; that there were on board a fire engine and hose as required by Congress; that they were stowed in a proper place; that sufficient reasons were shown why they were not available to fight the fire; and that there were three and a half dozen fire buckets on board. The company contended that the steering apparatus was good; that the loss of the boat did not result from not having steering wheel and tiller chains instead of ropes; and that the parting of the wheel ropes did not contribute to the loss.

The court documents show that an agreement was made on August 1, 1839, by William F. Harnden of Boston and Charles Handy, president of the New Jersey Steam Navigation Company, for Harnden to pay $250 per month to transport one wooden crate five feet by five feet in width and height and six feet in length once a day for the rest of the year. The contract stated that "the said crate, with its contents, is to be at all times exclusively at the risk of the said William F. Harnden; and the New Jersey Steam Navigation Company will not, in any event, be responsible, either to him or his employers, for the loss of any goods, wares, merchandise, money, notes, bills, evidences of debt, or property of any and every description." On December 31, the contract was renewed for one year from January 1, 1840.

The contract seemed to hold the steamboat company harmless for the loss of the coins and leave Harnden's company to make up for the loss. And on October 18, 1842, the District Court issued a pro forma decree dismissing the libel with costs awarded to the steamboat line.

The bank appealed to the Circuit Court, which heard the case in its November 1843 term. The appellate judges overturned the district court ruling, reasoning that a corporation engaged under legislative authority in the transportation of passengers and freight over navigable waters was "in the exercise of a sort of public office, and has public duties to perform."

The steamboat company appealed to the Supreme Court, contending that the circuit court decision should be reversed on several grounds:

> *That the contract…is not a contract within the admiralty and maritime jurisdiction of the courts of the United States; and hence that this court, sitting as a court of admiralty, has no jurisdiction of this cause. That, in fact, the* [bank] *did not deliver…the said gold and silver coin… but that the contract…was wholly with one William F. Harnden, a carrier and forwarder on his own account and risk, and…hence* [if the bank has]…*any cause of action for the loss of their said coin, it is against Harnden.…By virtue of this contract, Harnden was the*

insurer of his own crate.... Under these circumstances, we cannot be liable for any degree of negligence, or for want of sufficiency in our boat and equipments.

The justices ruled in *New Jersey Steam Navigation Company v. Merchants' Bank* on January 1, 1848, that the federal courts did have jurisdiction in the admiralty case under the Judiciary Act of 1789. They affirmed the appeals court rulings for the bank for the loss of the $14,000 in gold coins and $11,000 in silver coins.

The court recognized a carrier's right to limit its liability as a common carrier by contract, but it held the limitation could not be construed to extend to "willful misconduct, gross negligence, or want of ordinary care." Reviewing the record, the justices concluded that "there was a great want of care, and which amounted to gross negligence, on the part of the [company] in the stowage of cotton, especially regarding its exposure to fire from the covering of the boiler deck, and the casing of the steam chimney."

The justices said the company must pay the loss "with costs, and damages at the rate of six per centum per annum."[234]

The Supreme Court decision terrified the shipping industry. Faced with potentially huge damage claims on top of the cost of a lost vessel, the shipping lines looked to Congress for assistance. It would take three years to get it, but in 1851 Congress approved the Shipowners' Limitation of Liability Act of 1851.

The Supreme Court decision reconfirmed a long-standing rule of common law—that a common carrier transporting goods for the public was considered the insurer of those goods and was liable for any damage or loss except by an act of God or a "public enemy." That rule dated back to the Roman Empire, but over centuries, European maritime powers gradually chipped away at it to bolster their shipping industries. The Shipowners' Limitation of Liability Act modified the common law rule by limiting the liability of shipowners for damage to or loss of cargo unless it was caused by negligence.[235]

9

THE EARLY SALVAGE ATTEMPTS

I n the years that the courts and Congress were thrashing out liability and safety issues, there were multiple efforts to salvage the *Lexington* or some of its contents.

1840

The first attempts to locate the wreck and retrieve bodies and the most valuable cargo came two months after the sinking. At least one was authorized by freight transporter William F. Harnden, who had shipped the Merchants' Bank of Boston's $25,000 in coins.

"Captain Taylor left the city yesterday with his submarine armor [a diving suit], for the scene of the late terrible disaster, having been employed to search for the unrecovered bodies of the drowned, and also look for certain packages of money known to have been shipped by the *Lexington*," *The Corrector*, the weekly newspaper in Sag Harbor, wrote on March 7, reprinting an item from the *Boston Post*.

The newspaper followed up on April 1 with an item from the *Boston Courier*: "A letter has been received in this city, from Mr. Harnden's agent at New York, stating that Mr. Taylor, with his marine armor, has succeeded in finding the wreck of the *Lexington* after one day's search, and that a piece of the boat has been raised. This piece was found at the depth of 114 feet, and was heavily loaded with iron; probably a piece near the engine." There is no record of what became of that artifact.

Also on April 1, a letter by Captain Joseph Fuller dated March 26 was printed in the *New York Gazette*. It stated, "I left New York a week ago last Monday, in the sloop *Unity*, arrived at Stoney [Stony] Brook the same evening. The weather being very severe during the whole time since, we have not been able to make but one and a half days search. On Tuesday, we found a part of the hull, about 8 or 10 feet long. On the 25th all hands were discharged in consequence of the severity of the weather. Nothing further will be done till the weather moderates." There is no further record of additional searches that year.

1842

Two years after the initial salvage attempts, Harnden tried again, this time planning to raise the hulk rather than just retrieve valuables.

According to the *New York Journal of Commerce* on August 10, 1842,

> Divers have found the remains of this ill fated steamship, and have thoroughly examined the after part of the hold. The center was covered by a part of the bow, which had broken off near the engine and fallen over upon it. The men say that there is no sand in the ship, and nothing to prevent her being raised, though she lies in a hundred and twenty feet of water. It will be recollected that the iron chest on board the Lexington contained a large sum of money in specie [coins] and bank notes. So far no bodies have been discovered, and it is not probable that any remained on board when she went down. Arrangements are now making to raise her immediately.

On September 21, the newspaper reported that the salvors had recovered a package of $800 in bills from the wreck, according to the Harnden firm quoted in the *Boston Post*.

On September 24, the *Journal of Commerce* reprinted an item from the *New York Tribune* that noted that "the wreck of this ill-fated vessel has been raised to the surface of the water, but one of the chains breaking, she again sank in 120 feet of water. The attempt is again in progress. The eight hundred dollars recovered from her were not in bills, as before stated, but in a lump of silver, weighing 30 pounds, melted by fire, the box having been emptied on the deck to be used as a bucket for throwing water on the flames." The hull was not raised again.

1843

The primitive diving bell used by Mark W. Davis of Newark, New Jersey, in salvage attempts on the *Lexington* in 1843 and 1850 on display at Library Park in Harrison, New Jersey. *Tod Thonger photos.*

A year after bringing the charred wreckage of the *Lexington* to the surface only to lose it again, there was another salvage attempt.

"We understand that Mr. Mark W. Davis of Newark, descended in a diving bell on Monday last [May 22], and recovered part of the wreck of this unfortunate steamer, destruction of which caused such a lamentable loss of life," the *Brooklyn Evening Star* reported on May 26, 1843. "The remnants which have been recovered are said to be a great curiosity—portions of them being burned and charred. We hear that they will be brought to the city this morning for exhibition." *The Corrector* in Sag Harbor, reprinting an item from the *New York Express*, added on June 7 that Davis "succeeded in raising a piece weighing about six tons. Mr. George A. Wells, of the city, has it in his possession." The eighteen-by-eight-foot section of the steamboat raised after eight hours of work was placed on view at Castle Garden at the Battery in lower Manhattan where the public could view it for 12½ cents, the *New York Herald* reported on June 9. It is not known what became of this artifact.

1850

After a seven-year hiatus, salvor Mark Davis returned to the *Lexington* wreck in July 1850. The crew placed chains underneath the hulk but was unable to raise it, the *Brooklyn Daily Eagle* reported on August 2.

The next salvage attempt came in September. Albert D. Bishop, a marine engineer from Brooklyn, visited the site with his invention: "Bishop's Patent Floating Derrick." It used a system of pulleys and ropes to raise large objects from the bottom. Bishop dropped down to the wreck wearing a suit of "submarine armor" and found nothing aft of the steam engine and only about twenty feet of the forward deck, the *New-York Daily Tribune* reported on September 16. The steam engine and other mechanical equipment were so corroded by the salt water and rusted after a decade at the bottom of the Sound that they crumbled when touched. Bishop gave up any thoughts of salvage and returned home.

The final salvage attempt that year—and for 133 years—was made two months later. The *Tribune* reported on November 11 that J.E. McGowan of Boston used a "submarine armor and diving apparatus" to examine the wreckage and found it filled with mud and honeycombed with worm holes. On the sixteenth, the *Brooklyn Evening Star* wrote that "the operations on the wreck of the *Lexington*, sunk some years ago in the sound, have been somewhat successful. By means of the sub-marine armor and diving apparatus, a survey was made of the wreck, which lies in twenty-one fathoms [126 feet] of water. They are after the safe, which contains $80,000 in bills and gold." McGowan managed to recover an anchor, a cable left from an earlier salvage effort, some pieces of machinery and "some gold and copper, and human bones of the ill-fated passengers," the *Buffalo Daily Courier* noted on November 21.

A February 1, 1896 retrospective article in the *Long-Islander* in Huntington noted that "the boat had a safe aboard full of money, but this has never been found, although divers have gone down repeatedly for it. The boiler was raised and brought ashore at Crane Neck bend, where it now lies, nearly destroyed by the elements." This seems unlikely based on Bishop's description of the corrosion of metal parts of the wreck.

One artifact of the early salvage efforts is still in existence: Davis's diving bell. It is on display in Harrison, New Jersey, in western Hudson County. The diving bell was manufactured in 1812 by the Novelty Iron Works of Manhattan for an attempt to salvage the reported treasure in coins from the British frigate HMS *Hussar*, which struck a rock and sank at Hell Gate in the East River in 1780 during the American Revolution. Afterward, the bell was purchased by Joseph Tuers, a farmer in Harrison who displayed it on the banks of the Passaic River. In 1825, the farmer sold it for $5,000 to Hiram Davis, and Mark Davis (likely his son) used it to reach the wreckage of the *Lexington*. The diving bell remained with his family until there were no more descendants, at which point the Town of Harrison acquired it and put it on display in Library Park.[236]

After 1850, the *Lexington* was not visited again for 133 years until adventure author Clive Cussler decided to rediscover the location of the wreck. That story is told in chapter 12.

10

THE STEAMBOAT SAFETY LAWS

Despite the shocking loss of life and tremendous public interest and outcry over the *Lexington* disaster, demands that Congress take action to improve steamboat safety went unheeded for a dozen years. Then, finally, the lawmakers in Washington approved the Steamboat Safety Act of 1852.

Ever since the *Claremont* had proven the feasibility for commercial operation of steamboats in 1807, there had been a series of fires and boiler explosions around the country. In 1823 alone, 14 percent of all steam vessels in the United States were destroyed by explosions, resulting in more than one thousand fatalities.[237] These recurring disasters generated public outrage and demands for safety regulation. But while there was much debate in Congress, no legislation was enacted, even after President Martin Van Buren urged Congress to act in his State of the Union address in December 1837 following the explosion of the *Ben Sherrod* during a race with another steamboat on the Mississippi River that resulted in the deaths of more than 120 passengers and crew in May.[238]

Finally, three months after the *Moselle*'s boiler exploded on the Ohio River on April 25, 1838, with the deaths of at least 114 passengers, lawmakers took a first step toward regulating the safety practices of the industry by passing the Safety Act of 1838. The law, formally known as An Act to Provide for the Better Security of the Lives of Passengers on Board Vessels Propelled in Whole or in Part by Steam, created what eventually became the Steamboat Inspection Service as part of the Treasury Department.[239]

The lawmakers did not feel they had the expertise to set specific safety standards, so the act required only that steamboats be licensed and their boilers be inspected twice a year and hulls annually. It stipulated that separate inspectors for hulls and steam engines be appointed in each port by the local federal district court judge. Inspectors would use their own judgment as to whether the steamboats could operate safely. Their only renumeration was a five-dollar fee per inspection paid by the steamboat companies. There were also provisions to reduce the danger of fire, such as requiring a "fire engine" or water pump with a suction hose to be dropped overboard and mandating the use of iron rods or chains, rather than ropes, to link the steering wheel and tiller. The *Lexington* had been built with these rods, although they were connected to the steering wheel and tiller with rawhide ropes that burned through in the pilothouse, as noted previously.

It was soon apparent that there were significant loopholes in the act, as the fire on the *Lexington* demonstrated. Major ones were the failure to specify what type of testing should be done and the long intervals between inspections. Serious flaws could develop in the boilers in the six months between inspections. In addition, the federal judges designated to appoint inspectors had no expertise in the industry, making it difficult to weigh the qualifications of applicants. The inspectors were appointed for life, providing little accountability for poor job performance. The inspectors being dependent on their five-dollar inspection fees paid by the companies led to incompetent men being hired in some jurisdictions and competing to perform more inspections. In New York, at least, Bunker and Clark, who were appointed in September 1838, certainly were experienced in their trade and had a reputation for thoroughness, as brought out in the inquest. But nationwide, some steamboats inspected and certified by inspectors exploded soon afterward while others were condemned as unseaworthy by insurance companies.

Another major omission in the law was that it provided little means to enforce it or for preventing a vessel that failed inspection from operating. The act provided for the judicial system to enforce seven of its provisions, such as operating without a license or navigation lights, with penalties for noncompliance. But the steamboat companies had to be sued by the government in federal court to collect the penalties. And while the inspectors would receive half of the fine in a successful prosecution, the enforcement process was so laborious and time-consuming that the inspectors rarely bothered to initiate legal action. During the fourteen years the act was in effect, there were only twenty-five prosecutions for noncompliance. Convictions were obtained in fewer than half of these cases, and the judges who exonerated the companies sometimes questioned the constitutionality of the law.

Besides the provisions that could result in fines for noncompliance, the law also allowed for criminal and civil cases to be brought against the companies. Despite the continuing spate of fatal accidents, the first criminal prosecution case was not tried until 1848 and the first civil case three years after that. In the criminal cases, it was extremely difficult for prosecutors to prove guilt to achieve a manslaughter conviction specified in the law and subject to up to ten years in prison. The technology of the steamboats was so complex that proving human negligence versus machinery failure was often impossible. The act placed the burden on steamboat operators subject to a lawsuit to prove that they were not negligent, which was nearly impossible to do. Fortunately for the companies, they were rarely sued because there was no provision for the relatives of those killed to do so. Only those injured could file suit, and there were usually more deaths than injuries when a boiler exploded.[240]

With so many of his constituents killed on the *Lexington*, Massachusetts senator Daniel Webster introduced a resolution on January 27, 1840, two weeks after the sinking, that would require the Committee on Commerce to investigate whether the Safety Act of 1838 needed to be strengthened. By March, Senator John Ruggles of Maine had introduced a bill to amend the 1838 act, including banning the burning of coal unless the steamboat's furnace, flues and smoke pipes were certified as properly suitable for that fuel. The proposed legislation also would have established specific procedures for testing boilers, including the use of hydrostatic pressure testing.

The industry pushed back strongly against the measure. A group of owners, including the New Jersey Steam Navigation Company, submitted a sixty-four-page document titled "Memorial of Sundry Proprietors and Managers of American Steamvessels, on the Impolicy and Injustice of Certain Enactments Contained in the Law Relating to Steamboats, and Asking to Be Restored to the Rights and Privileges Which Belong to Other Citizens Engaged in Navigation." This opus argued that the Safety Act of 1838 already placed requirements on the steamboat operators beyond those imposed on other industries and that it could drive them out of business. The counterattack worked; the legislation died.

The result of the weak 1838 law was that in the decade after its enactment, the number of explosions remained about the same, and injuries and property loss increased, although fatalities decreased. The increases came even while the number of steamboat trips dropped because of a poor economy and a drought that lowered rivers, reducing the ability of steamboats to travel.[241]

Because of the problems with the 1838 act, there was continued pressure on the federal government to improve the regulation system. But Congress was leery of plugging the loopholes in the absence of Supreme Court rulings clarifying whether the federal government or the states had the constitutional right to regulate steamboat operations. The lawmakers were also hesitant about interfering with the economic benefits provided by the booming private companies, preferring to let the industry regulate itself and make improvements to satisfy public demands.

But by 1852, the situation had changed. Congress was finally convinced of its ability to regulate the industry because of the Supreme Court's expansive view of the federal government's authority to regulate interstate commerce. And public pressure to make steamboat travel safer was unabated after accidents such as the destruction of the *G.P. Griffith* in June 1851 on Lake Erie with the deaths of 250 of the 300 onboard and the *Henry Clay* on the Hudson River off Yonkers in 1852 with 80 fatalities.

The Safety Act of 1852 amended the earlier statute by creating a national network of steamboat inspectors overseen by a board of nine regional supervising inspectors appointed by the president. The port inspectors were appointed by a committee consisting of the customs collector, district court judge and supervising inspector for their port. They were now paid salaries by the government rather than fees by the steamboat companies. In addition to the annual inspections, they were authorized to board vessels in their ports at any time to check for compliance. The local inspectors, acting as a board, were responsible for licensing engineers and pilots as well as hearing appeals by steamboat operators on citations issued. These boards were given the authority to summon witnesses and suspend and revoke licenses.

The amended law established standards for inspections, including annual hydrostatic boiler pressure inspections at one and one-half times their working pressure. There were requirements for two safety pressure release valves, water and pressure gauges and devices to ensure that the water level in the boiler never dropped to less than four inches above the flue. Boiler plates were required to be at least one-quarter of an inch thick, made of high-quality iron and stamped by the manufacturers in a place visible to inspectors. It also required specific safety equipment and banned explosive or flammable cargo without a special license. Cotton was not mentioned, likely because of its economic importance to southern growers and northeastern mill owners.

As was the case under the Act of 1838, most of the requirements of the new law were backed by monetary penalties and even occasional prison sentences. The provision for prosecuting manslaughter cases was retained from the earlier law, but the civil liability provision was amended to allow surviving passengers to sue for personal injuries or damage to property. Inspectors were now subject to liability under the act. Supervising inspectors were held responsible for reporting malfeasance by inspectors to the secretary of the treasury for investigation and possible removal. Bribery and issuing false certificates of inspection were punishable by six months in prison and a $500 fine.[242]

When the new regulations took effect on January 1, 1853, they had an immediate impact. The new steamboat inspection agency began publishing notices in the newspapers about suspending or revoking steamboat officers' licenses and refusing to grant licenses to vessels. There were trials of officers involved in accidents. Between 1860 and 1875, more than 750 engineer and pilot licenses were revoked. The amended law resulted in a significant drop in the number of steamboat fatalities. In 1853, there were only 45 fatalities compared to 1,038 in 1851. There were 33 percent fewer deaths in the first eight years after passage of the new regulations than in the same period prior to enactment of the law.[243]

But while the 1852 law did reduce the number of steamboat accidents, it did not eliminate them. In 1858, the *Pennsylvania* exploded on the Mississippi River, killing more than 250. More than 1,700 died when boilers on the overloaded *Sultana* exploded on the Mississippi in 1865 as it was transporting freed Union prisoners north at the end of the Civil War.

Because of disasters like these, Congress continued to debate the need for increased scrutiny of the industry after the war. Proposals to toughen the 1852 law initially were thwarted by southern lawmakers who resisted provisions that singled out cargoes of cotton for additional precautions.

Eventually, the Safety Act of 1871 was enacted. It created an Office of the Supervising Inspector General, which was given the responsibility of overseeing what became the Steamboat Inspection Service. It established certifying requirements for vessels, pilots and engineers. The law established specifications for iron and steel plates used in boilers and required they be inspected annually. All steamboats were required to carry firefighting equipment that included fire extinguishers, fire buckets, water barrels and axes. There had to be a life jacket for every passenger. The steering gear on any steamboat carrying passengers had to use wire tiller ropes or iron rods or chains. And additional precautions were required for any steamboat transporting cotton.[244]

11

REDISCOVERING THE WRECK

In the decades after the sinking and the ill-fated salvage attempts, most people forgot about the *Lexington*. But not all maritime history buffs, particularly a prominent one: best-selling adventure novelist Clive Cussler. When he wasn't writing novels such as *Raise the Titanic*, Cussler was investing some of his immense royalty income in searching for famous undiscovered shipwrecks, some of them featured prominently in his works. Cussler always said he was more interested in the history of the wrecks than exploiting them for profit. His team would only recover a few artifacts to help identify the vessels and then donate the items to museums. The always colorful author organized his wreck expeditions through a nonprofit search organization he created called the National Underwater and Marine Agency (NUMA), the same agency he created as the employer for the heroes in some of his novels.

Because the *Lexington* had been built by Cornelius Vanderbilt as a showpiece and then ended up as the worst maritime disaster in the history of Long Island, the vessel earned a place on Cussler's wish list. He set out to find it in 1982.

The author described the search in one of his rare nonfiction books, *The Sea Hunters*, published in 1996. Cussler wrote that the idea of searching for the *Lexington* came from Bob Fleming, a respected Washington, D.C. shipwreck scholar who had worked with him on a regular basis. He hired Margaret Dubitsky, "a Long Island schoolteacher, who worked long and hard in compiling a remarkable research package from New York State and local archives." But that remarkable research almost scuttled the expedition before it started because she found references that said the steamboat had been raised. "One vague report claimed it was brought to the surface and towed away, suggesting it no longer lay on the bottom of the Sound," Cussler wrote. "It was known that occasional sea hunts through the decades have failed to find a trace of the steamboat. Could this explain why she was never located by either sport divers or fishermen?"[245]

But the writer added, "I hated to give up on her. Much of my life people have told me I was wasting my time or engaging in an exercise in futility when I tackled a seemingly hopeless project. What is interesting is that they were right only 40 percent of the time." Cussler doubted that the wreck had been successfully salvaged. "Raising a two-hundred-foot vessel from 130 feet of water is a feat rarely if ever attempted today," he wrote. Between difficulties with weather, unpredictable seas and the heavy lifting equipment involved, the expense can be enormous, he noted.

> *Having the technology in 1842 to accomplish such an undertaking seems incredible. Hard-hat diving was in its infancy. Decompression tables were unknown. Did divers sling chains under the hull to lift her out of the water, or were cables dragged under the wreck by two vessels steaming side by side? And then there had to be a barge and a crane with the capacity to lift a 488-ton vessel to the surface. Even by twenty-first-century standards this takes a derrick almost the size of the one used by the* Glomar Explorer *to raise the Russian submarine K-129 from the floor of the Pacific Ocean in 1974.*[246]

As detailed in chapter 9, despite these obstacles, the *Lexington* was almost raised to the surface in 1842 before one of the lifting cables snapped and the hulk fell back to the bottom of the Sound in pieces.

Because his researcher turned up no insurance company or other contemporary records documenting a successful salvage operation, Cussler said, "I forged ahead and formed an expedition to search for the wreckage I felt certain was still on the seabed. I was told by any number of divers that I was laboring in vain and pouring time and money into a sinkhole."

Nonetheless, Zeff Loria of Port Jefferson agreed to serve as the project manager. He and Cussler analyzed the material gathered in the research to try to figure out where to search. "Of all the sightings from witnesses on shore, I placed my faith in the Old Field lighthouse keeper, who reported seeing the flames die about four miles north of the Point and slightly to the west. Figuring that he was a good judge of distance across water, I laid out an initial grid of four square miles in his approximate area, and the search was on."

The group began by doing a general survey of tide, bottom conditions and visibility over a sunken barge in the area using Captain Tony Bresnah's dive boat *Day Off*. "One to two feet of visibility was not unexpected, but the current was much stronger than estimated," Cussler wrote. "We figured close to four knots [4.6 miles per hour], and all divers were holding on to the anchor chain while stretched horizontal like flags in a windstorm." To complicate matters, it turned out that half of their search grid lay under the route of the Bridgeport–Port Jefferson ferries.[247]

For the second dive the following year, the team went out with Captain Mike Arnell on the *Mikado III* and deployed a gradiometer to detect the presence of iron and site-scan sonar to record any objects rising above the floor of the Sound. They used a LORAN navigational unit to keep track of their position. Unlike most searches for shipwrecks, this one did not take long to pay off. Sonar technician Tom Cummings found three solid targets in the first hour of the search that appeared to be one large vessel broken into three sections, one of which included the *Lexington* engine's walking beam and a large section of a paddlewheel guard.[248] The expedition determined that the lighthouse keeper on Old Field Point was fairly accurate in his estimation of where he saw the flames because the team found the wreck three and a half miles north and slightly west of his location.

In the initial hardcover edition of the book, Cussler wrote that divers from his team went over the side and headed down the anchor line. "The view inside a tunnel offered better visibility," Cussler said. "With powerful lights and a safety line, the divers made narrow sweeps of the central section of the wreck. With bottom time restricted to only ten minutes, major exploration was severely limited. The divers brought up a few bolts and pieces of charred wood. They reported seeing one of the paddlewheels and more charred timbers and described the whole construction as looking like an egg crate, verifying a match to the *Lexington*'s unusual box frame."

But there was a problem with this description. Cussler wasn't aboard and relied on project manager Zeff Loria to provide a play-by-play description for the book—and the description was far from accurate. In reality, only one diver made it down to the *Lexington*, and he wasn't initially part of Cussler's team. It was Robert Wass, a Long Island commercial diver and dive shop owner who talked his way onto the team after tracking down Cussler at his Manhattan hotel.

Wass, then only twenty-four, told the author of this book in an interview at his Smithtown home that "I was always diving as a kid. In 1981 I decided to go to commercial deep diving school." He trained at one on the South

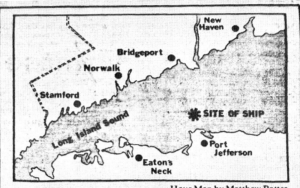

Hour Map by Matthew Potter

Right: An article in *The Hour* from Norwalk, Connecticut, describes the rediscovery of the *Lexington* in 1983 by an expedition organized by adventure author Clive Cussler. *Courtesy of Hearst Communications Inc.*

Below: Charred wood from the *Lexington* recovered by diver Robert Wass in 1983 was donated to the Suffolk County Vanderbilt Museum. *Courtesy of the Suffolk County Vanderbilt Museum.*

Ship Employed by Vanderbilt Found on L.I. Sound Bottom

NEW YORK (AP) — A ship that helped start the Vanderbilt family fortune and sank in a spectacular fire which killed 150 people has been found on the bottom of Long Island Sound, says the head of a group that searched for the wreck.

Clive Cussler, author of the book "Raise The Titanic!" and leader of a non-profit group that hunts shipwrecks, the National Underwater and Marine Agency Inc., announced the discovery Tuesday.

Janet Warner, a staff worker at the Vanderbilt Museum in Centerport, N.Y., said details of the find match the Lexington, a cargo-passenger ship which Commodore Cornelius Vanderbilt built in 1835 and sold three years later to the Stonington Line.

Pieces of charred wood have been raised, but $100,000 worth of silver coins found aboard have not yet been brought to the surface.

The wreck, resting upright in three sections in about 80 feet of water, was found between the towns of Port Jefferson and Stony Brook, the discoverers said.

Please See Page 8

THE HOUR 10/12/83
PAGE 1 & 8.

Continued from page 1
Cussler said several pre-Civil War artifacts found on the ship will be donated to the Vanderbilt Museum.

Shore of Long Island where by 1983 he was certified in the use of mixed gases, hardhat diving and underwater welding and had learned to take photographs and video. "I loved it, and I was interested in deep diving and visiting wrecks," he said. Then he was trained as an instructor in California by the Professional Association of Dive Instructors and was hired to teach at a dive shop in Brooklyn before he opened his own dive shop on Long Island called Island Divers.

When Wass read in the newspapers about Cussler's plans to rediscover the *Lexington*, "I found his hotel in New York City and I called him. I said 'Clive, you don't know who I am but I have a dive shop in Bay Shore and I have access to divers and anything you would need including lifting equipment, you name it. If you put me on top of the *Lexington*, I'll find it."

Wass said Cussler was skeptical but finally told him to meet the crew the next morning at the dock in Port Jefferson. Wass asked if he could bring an experienced deep diver he trusted named Chris Lafferty. "He said, 'No, out of the question. I have four really good divers here so it will be no problem.'"

Wass was leery so he arranged for three divers from the Northport Fire Department he had trained to follow Cussler's boat out to keep an eye on things. One of them, Tod Thonger, who already had a longtime interest in the *Lexington*, told the author of this book that "we trailered a boat to Port Jefferson and followed them out. We were about a quarter of a mile away and watched what was going on."

Thonger explained, "I got into the *Lexington* when I was growing up, about twelve years old, on Eatons Neck," the closest point of land when the fire was discovered on the steamboat. "My parents had a lot of books, including one on Currier & Ives. I remember thumbing through the book and I ran across the image of the burning of the *Lexington* and on the bottom of the image there was a map of Long Island Sound and that caught my eye. That's one of the reasons I got interested in scuba diving." He began collecting documents and images, including five original lithographs, three decades ago because "it's the biggest thing that ever happened on the North Shore of Long Island." On vacations, he visits the graves or memorials to victims of the steamboat fire. As of the fall of 2022, he had been to twenty-five of the thirty-one graves of victims and survivors he has identified.

During the 1983 expedition, Wass said his concerns about the quality of the divers assembled by Cussler were quickly validated. "At six o'clock in the morning, I meet these three divers and I'm not impressed at all," he related. "These guys couldn't go down 150 feet." They had only single compressed air tanks without smaller backup "pony bottle" tanks, backup regulators or

Lexington researcher and collector Tod Thonger at his home on Long Island with his research binders and four original prints of the steamboat on the wall behind him. *Author photo.*

other safety equipment. When they admitted they had tried to reach the wreck before and failed, Wass told them, "When we get down there, I'm going on my own."

"In the Sound, there is zero light below fifty feet because of the silt," Wass explained. "When you get down there, it's very quiet and very dark with four feet of visibility. I had three tanks with me, and I go sliding down the anchor line taking pictures of these guys. At thirty or forty feet, they had problems equalizing [their ears] and every problem in the world." He didn't have time to wait for the other divers, whom he considered unqualified amateurs. "Goodbye, and I took off." Wass calculated he could only remain on the wreck about ten minutes without major decompression "hangs" on the way up to eliminate nitrogen from his body so he would not get decompression sickness, commonly called "the bends." He ended up spending about twenty-five minutes descending and exploring and about thirty minutes ascending and decompressing.

The section of the *Lexington* he landed on—he is still unsure whether it was the bow or the stern—was in a depression scoured out by the current so his depth gauge showed a maximum depth of 152 feet. "I get down and I took a picture of the anchor hooked into the wreck. I start looking around. I saw weird colored wire, copper color," probably the remains of the copper cables used to raise the wreck to the surface in 1842. "I want something that says *Lexington* on it. I'm looking all around and I'm not going to go back empty-handed. So I found a big piece of wood that I had to snap off and I had a 250-pound lift bag [a vinyl bag that can be filled with air from a regulator to raise heavy objects up to the specified weight capacity for each bag] and I hooked it to it." He didn't have time to go back to and up the anchor line so he sent the lift bag and the wood up from where he was and began his slow ascent under the bag with safety stops at twenty and ten feet from the surface.

Because of the strong current, when Wass surfaced he found that he was about a mile from the anchored dive boat. When the boat picked him up, the other divers told him they thought he had drowned on the wreck. They recovered the lift bag and piece of charred wood. The wood that Wass brought up was turned over to Cussler as previously agreed. The author sent samples to the Woods Hole Oceanographic Institute in Massachusetts, which determined it was from the *Lexington*.

The rediscovery of the remains of the *Lexington* made front-page headlines. The *New York Times* reported on October 12, 1983, that Cussler's team claimed to have found "the wreck of Commodore Cornelius Vanderbilt's elegant, silver-laden passenger and cargo ship," inaccurately describing the ship as still belonging to Vanderbilt.[249] Cussler told the newspaper that his research showed the ship had been carrying $20,000 in bills and between $18,000 and $40,000 in silver coins when it sank. The money was "in buckets right out on the deck," Cussler told the reporter. "I guess they could trust people more then. Today it's over $100,000 worth of silver." But Wass recovered no silver because most of it had been thrown over the side so crew and passengers could use the containers to throw water on the fire or had been brought up by the early salvage efforts.

Cussler and Wass both wanted to return to the shipwreck, but the diver said that later "I talked to Cussler on the phone and he promised to go diving there again and he wanted me to lead the team but everything started falling apart." Cussler's team never returned to the site.

But Wass said, "I went back with my own people a couple of times. It was really discouraging" because without state-of-the-art lighting, he could see very little of the hulk. He said the visibility in the dark water was so bad that, despite what Cussler had written based on Loria's description, he could not make out much detail of the vessel except a glimpse of its iconic latticework structure. "It's real dangerous, and not for everybody. It's cold and dark, and I've seen people bug out in conditions better than that." On one of his subsequent dives, Wass recovered another piece of wood with a bronze spike running through it that he displays in his house.

Wass said Cussler promised he would be credited for reaching the wreck when he wrote *The Sea Hunters*. But it did not happen, at least initially. "When the hardcover book came out, my father gave me a copy for Christmas and said, 'Here's the wreck you did.' But I'm not in it." The book credited another diver who never made it to the bottom for recovering the artifacts because the information was given to the author by Zeff Loria. So Wass said, "I made some calls." He talked to the publisher, Simon & Schuster, and Cussler, who said he learned the true story after publication. "He did come through, and I got into the paperback [edition] where he changed it all," Wass said.

In the paperback, Cussler revised the description of how the dive came about to credit Wass, although it still wasn't completely accurate, according to Wass. The revised version says:

> *For the second attempt, Zeff Loria assembled a first-rate crew. The* Mikado III, *captained by Mike Arnell, an experienced divemaster, was chartered. The dive team was led by Robert Wass along with Doug Rutledge and Sandy Zicaro. Equipment included a Schonstedt radiometer to detect the presence of iron, a Klein Associates Inc. side scan sonar to record objects protruding from the sea bottom, and a LORAN navigation unit, since made obsolete by newer Global Positioning Systems, using satellites. For once the tedium of running search lanes did not cause uncontrolled yawning. Tom Cummings, Klein's sonar technician, announced not one but three solid targets the first hour into the search. Subsequent runs over the target suggested one large vessel broken into three sections.*

On one run, Cussler wrote, the sonar recorded the steam engine's walking beam and a large section of a paddlewheel guard, but Wass never saw them. "Captain Mike Arnell then expertly moored the *Mikado III* directly over the wreck so the divers could descend on the anchor line. The bottom depth registered 140 feet on the boat's echo sounder and the divers' depth gauges." But only Wass got that deep. "This time we waited for slack tide. The view inside a tunnel offered better visibility than what Wass found on the bottom, and they had to examine the wreck with powerful underwater lights." Cussler's reference to "they" was probably a typo left over from the initial version because earlier he makes it clear that only Wass made it to the

 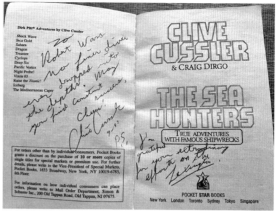

Diver Robert Wass at his Long Island home holding a paperback copy of Clive Cussler's book describing the rediscovery of the *Lexington* and the inscription from Cussler crediting Wass for finding the wreck. *Author photo.*

wreck. Cussler's description also makes it sound like the writer was on the boat, when he was not. "Using a safety line, we made narrow sweeps of the central section of the wreckage," Cussler wrote. "With the divers restricted to only 10 minutes of bottom time, major exploration was severely limited. Wass brought up a few bolts and pieces of charred wood. He reported seeing one of the paddle wheels and more charred timbers and described the whole construction as looking like an egg crate, verifying the *Lexington*'s unusual box frame." Wass differs, saying he couldn't tell what he was looking at except a bit of the box-like construction because of the poor visibility, and he never saw a paddlewheel.

Cussler summed up his feelings about the steamboat by saying:

> *It is a pity you cannot stand on the sandy bottom, step back, and view the wreckage in its entirety. The length of the burned and broken hull, the great paddle wheels, the walking beams of the engines are more imagined than seen. The dismal green, murky water allows you only a few close-up glimpses of how the ship must have once appeared. You feel as if you're groping through a haunted house in the dead of night.*
>
> *Because of the many long hours of research, I felt as though I had walked the decks of the* Lexington, *watched the smoke pour into the sky from her smokestack, seen her passengers and crew. To the other divers, she was simply a pile of debris on the bottom. I saw her in my mind as she once was, a greyhound of the waters. And yet I was not sorry to leave her.*

Cussler wrote that Robert Baldwin, a leading expert in wood science, identified the charred section of plank recovered by Wass as yellow pine, one of the woods used in the construction of the steamboat. "Wass also described strands of weird green wire that looped around the wreck. Believing that the wreck was raised before breaking into three pieces, I did a bit of detective work by contacting Mr. Oliver Bennett, an executive with a wire cable company." Cussler learned that in 1840 the technology did not allow fabrication of flexible solid wire cable so that companies at the time used iron strands woven around a core of copper to make flexible wire. The writer concluded that after a century and a half in salt water, the iron in the cables had rusted away, leaving only the copper covered with a green patina.[250]

The charred pieces of wood recovered were donated to the Suffolk County Vanderbilt Museum in Centerport. Then in 1989, that museum loaned them to the Maritime Industry Museum at the State University of New York Maritime College at Fort Schuyler in the Bronx. They are currently not on public display.[251]

After the paperback edition of *The Sea Hunters* was published, Cussler sent an inscribed copy to Wass. It said: "To Robert Wass—no finer diver ever dropped into the depths. May you find constant success. Cheers! Clive Cussler. 9-87. P.S. I'm grateful for your extraordinary effort on the *Lexington*."

Wass continued diving professionally. Within a year, he took a job with a commercial diving company on City Island in the Bronx. He changed jobs over the years but has remained a commercial diver, although he now does it sporadically "more for fun." He also worked as an electrical engineer and licensed electrician but has retired from that. Since 1982, Wass has served as a technical expert on diving accidents for medical examiners and attorneys on Long Island and in the New York metropolitan area. His biggest underwater achievement came on April 24, 1999, when he became the first person to dive under the thick ice at the geographic North Pole, an achievement chronicled in numerous magazines. "It's the most incredible thing I've ever done," he said.

12

THE *LEXINGTON* TODAY

Since Clive Cussler's team rediscovered the *Lexington* in 1983, experienced wreck divers have visited the site periodically. They have taken grainy and fuzzy still photographs and videos in the murky water, but no one had gotten a clear image of the steamboat since it sank—until 2020.

That's when diver and amateur historian Ben Roberts conducted a side-scan sonar documentation of Long Island Sound's most important shipwreck. The use of sound waves bouncing off the bottom to create an extremely clear image was part of an ongoing project undertaken by the then thirty-seven-year-old freelance executive consultant from Amagansett on Long Island's South Fork to document as many of the thousands of shipwrecks in the waters around Long Island and off the New Jersey coast as possible.

Roberts, who in 2018 with longtime dive buddy Alex Barnard created a company called Eastern Search & Survey,[252] in May 2020 spent half a day searching the waters west of the Stratford Shoal Lighthouse and north of Port Jefferson to produce what is believed to be the only scans of the ship in recent decades. The images show the hull—broken into two pieces after the failed 1842 salvage attempt—and one of its two detached paddlewheels in startling clarity.

"At the end of the day, I'm very certain I found the bow section—about 115 feet long—in 125 feet of water and a paddlewheel in about 80 feet of water," Roberts said. "We also found some uncharted wreckage not far from the bow section in 80 feet of water that looks to be about the right size—85

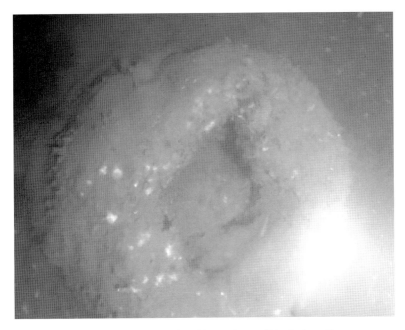

Photograph of a round object on the shipwreck, possibly the base for a mast, taken by diver John Beninati, formerly of Long Island and now a North Carolina resident, in 2013. *Copyright John Beninati.*

The dashboard of Ben Roberts's boat showing the side-scan sonar screen image of the *Lexington* wreckage. *Courtesy of Ben Roberts.*

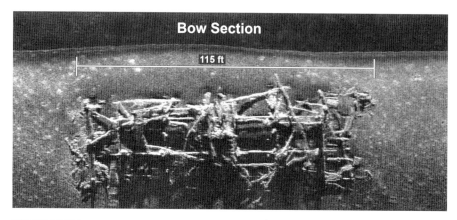

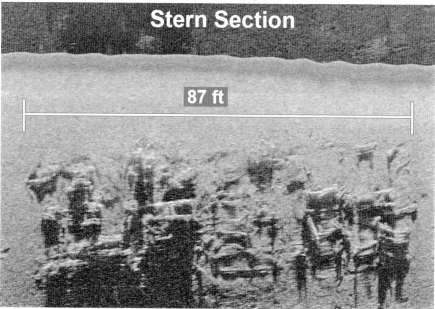

Top: Side-scan sonar image by Ben Roberts of the bow section of the *Lexington*. *Courtesy of Ben Roberts.*

Bottom: Side-scan sonar image of the stern section. *Courtesy of Ben Roberts.*

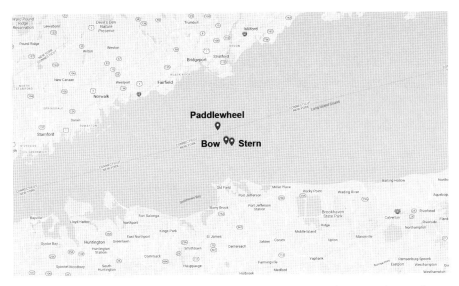

Map prepared by Ben Roberts showing the locations of the bow and stern sections and one paddlewheel from the *Lexington. Courtesy of Ben Roberts.*

feet—age and deterioration and construction style to possibly be the stern section." As for the missing second paddlewheel, Roberts, who moved to Virginia Beach, Virginia, in December 2021, said, "I think it's probably gone."

The scans appear more like latticework than a traditional shipwreck profile, which reflects Vanderbilt's unusual box-like design. Said Roberts: "It doesn't look like any other wreck that I've scanned."[253]

In the twentieth century, improved propulsion systems, navigation devices and safety equipment made major maritime disasters like the fire and sinking of the *Lexington* and collisions and groundings of other steamboats a rarity.

Most travelers today—driving on highways, crossing bridges or taking modern ferryboats—are unaware of the role that Long Island Sound played in developing the region's transportation system and some of the calamities experienced during that history. But it's important not to forget the sacrifice made by up to 146 people on the *Lexington* and others on different vessels so that travel by water could become fast as well as safe.

APPENDIX

This list of the identified *Lexington* passengers and crew members was compiled for the inquest jury and by publishers H.H. Brown and A.H. Stillwell in 1840 and amended in later published reports and by the research of amateur *Lexington* historian Tod Thonger. (The Black crew members were identified as "colored" at the time.) There are 150 people listed, but some of them may have been counted twice, initially unnamed and then later identified.

*Survivor
**One of the fifteen bodies recovered

PASSENGERS

Mr. Ballou or Bullard, New York, NY
Lydia Bates**, her daughter Lydia C. Bates and son James C. Bates,** New Jersey
Robert Blake, Wrentham, MA. President of Wrentham Bank. Memorial located in Wrentham Center Cemetery
Charles Boswell, NY
Mr. Bosworth, Royalton, VT
Charles Bracket, New York, NY. Clerk with N. Bracket **
Mr. H.C. Bradford, Boston, MA
Elias Brown Jr., Providence, RI
James Griswold Brown, Boston. Firm of Shall & Brown

John Brown, Boston. Memorial stone at Mount Auburn Cemetery, Cambridge, MA

John Brown, "a colored man"

Mr. Carey, New York

Captain Ichabod D. Carver, Providence, RI. Barque *Brontes*. Returning home to be married.

Royal T. Church, Baltimore, MD

John Corey, Foxborough, MA. Memorial stone in Mount Pleasant Cemetery, Taunton, MA

William Cowen or Cowan, New York, NY

Mr. H.C. Craig, New York, NY. Firm of Maitland, Kennedy & Company **

Jonathan G. Davenport, Middletown, CT. On his way home to be married.

Isaac Davis, Boston

William Dexter, Boston

Mr. Richard W. Dow, New York, NY. Firm of Dow & Company, Brooklyn

Nemiah F. Dyer, Pittsburgh, PA. Memorial stone in Pond Street Cemetery near Quincy, MA

Charles L. Eberle, "of the Theatre." A memorial is located in Union Cemetery in Brockton, MA

John Everett Jr., Boston. Returning from burial of a brother who had died recently in New York. Memorial stone in Old Village Cemetery near Quincy, MA ***

Jonathan Porter Felt Jr., Salem, MA. Memorial stone at Harmony Grove Cemetery, Salem

Henry James Finn, Canada. Popular playwright and comic actor

Rev. Dr. Charles Follen, Boston. Harvard professor and antislavery activist hired as the first preacher at the Free Christian Church in East Lexington, Massachusetts. He died in the *Lexington* disaster on his way to the dedication of a new church. A monument to him was erected in 1915 on the grounds of the church—now named Follen Church.

Captain Benjamin Foster, Providence

Alexander H. Fowler, New York, NY. An organ maker.

John Gordon, seaman of Cambridgeport, MA

Memorial stone for passenger John Corey in Mount Pleasant Cemetery in Taunton, Massachusetts. *Tod Thonger photo.*

Passenger Nemiah F. Dyer's memorial stone in the Pond Street Cemetery near Quincy, Massachusetts. *Tod Thonger photo.*

The plaque on the memorial for Charles Follen at the Follen Church in East Lexington, Massachusetts. *Tod Thonger photo.*

David Greene, Philadelphia **

Captain William A. Greene, Providence. Agent of Minot Shoe Company of Maine. ** Grave in North Burial Ground in Providence

Albert E. Harding, New York. Firm of Harding & Company

Adolphus Harnden, New York, NY. Superintendent of Harden's Express transporting bills and coins to Boston

Samuel Henry, Manchester, England. Firm of S. & A. Henry

Captain Chester Hillard, Fort Ann, NY. * Buried in Yantic Cemetery in Norwich, CT

Noah Hinckley, Portland, ME

Nathaniel Hobart, Boston. Memorial plaque at Mount Auburn Cemetery, Cambridge, MA.

Benjamin D. Holmes, Boston

Abraham Howard, Boston. Firm of Howard & Mersay

John Hoyt, Boston. Mail contractor

Thomas James, New York. A tailor

Mrs. Russell Jarvis and daughters, 8 and 12, New York

Joshua Johnson, Providence. "Colored man"

John W. Kerle, Baltimore, MD

Captain Eben J. Kimball, Salem, MA

Hezekiah Lawrence, New York, NY. Firm of Kelly & Lawrence

John A. Leach, Boston. Firm of Leach & Lovejoy **

Charles Lee, Boston. Memorial stone in Lee Family Cemetery, Barre, MA

John Lemist, Roxbury, MA. Treasurer of the Boston Leather Company

Jonathan Linfield, Stoughton, MA. Memorial in Pearl Street Cemetery

Capt. John Gorham Low, Boston. Agent of Boston Insurance Company. Memorial stone at First Parish Burial Grounds, Gloucester, MA

T.H.M. Lyon, Boston

John Martin and son Gilbert, England

Alphonso Mason, surveyor of the port of Gloucester, MA, and owner of the Gloucester Hotel. Memorial marker in Walton Cemetery, Lowell, MA

Captain Mattison

David McFarlane, mate of the brig *Clarion*

Patrick McKenna, New York

William Nichols, "(colored) of Providence"

Charles S. Noyes, New York, NY. Clerk with C.B. Babcock, New York. Nephew of victim Charles Phelps. Memorial stone at Evergreen Cemetery, Stonington

Memorial stone for passenger Alphonso Mason in the Walton Cemetery in Lowell, Massachusetts. *Tod Thonger photo.*

Mr. E.B. Patten, New York, NY

Mr. Peck, Stonington, CT

Charles H. Phelps, Stonington. Memorial stone at Evergreen Cemetery, Stonington

Mr. Phipps or Philips, New York

Richard Picket, Newburyport, MA. Clerk with Marquand & Company

Mr. Pierce, Portland, ME. Mate of the barque *Brontes*

Richard Pierpont, New York

William Price, Portland, ME

James Ray, Kennebunk, ME

Mr. Jean Ricker, Monroe, ME

Mary Russell, Stonington, CT. She was married one day earlier.

Robert Schultz, New York, NY

Mr. J.L. Sheaf, NY

George Brown Smith, Brooklyn, NY

Captain Theophilus Smith, Dartmouth, MA. Memorial at Methodist Cemetery in Dartmouth.

John G. Stone, Boston

Mr. Stuyvesant, Boston or New York

George O. Swan, Columbus, OH. Memorial stone in Green-Wood Cemetery, Brooklyn.

William Symes, "a colored boy of N.Y."

William H. Townsend, New York

Philo Upson, Egremont, MA. Contractor. ** Buried in Mount Everett Cemetery, Egremont

Mr. Van Cott, Stonington

Harrison Josiah Otis Walker, Baltimore. Memorial in South Cemetery in Belchertown, MA.

James Walker, seaman of Cambridgeport, MA

Mr. Warner, New York, NY

Stephen Waterbury, New York, NY. Firm of Mead & Waterbury, 25 Cedar Street.**

Justus Weston, Baltimore. Firm of Weston & Pendexter. Memorial stone at Laurel Hill Cemetery, Reading, MA.

Miss Sophia T. Wheeler, Greenfield, MA. Returning home to be married.**

The memorial marker for Captain Theophilus Smith, a *Lexington* passenger, in the Methodist Cemetery in Dartmouth, Massachusetts. *Tod Thonger photo.*

Passenger Justus Weston memorial at Laurel Hill Cemetery in Reading, Massachusetts. *Tod Thonger photo.*

Thomas White, Boston. Firm of Sands & White

Robert Williams, Cold Spring, NY

William H. Wilson, of Williamsburg, Brooklyn

Alice Pickering Winslow, New York, NY. Widow of Henry A. Winslow, whose body was being transported on the *Lexington* for burial. Memorial in Grove Hill Cemetery near Waltham, MA

John L. Winslow, Providence. Firm of D.L. & J. Winslow. Alice's father-in-law

William Winslow, Providence. Three members of the Winslow family were traveling to Providence with the body of Henry A. Winslow for his burial. They included his widow Alice. Memorial gravestone for the family members is at Grove Hill Cemetery, Waltham, MA.

A son of Charles Woodward, Philadelphia

Benjamin ——, Boston

William, a boy, England

Charles W. Woolsey, Boston. Sugar refiner. Memorial stone in private Woolsey Cemetery in Glen Cove, NY

CREW

Danial Aldridge, waiter, colored

Solomon Ashons, waiter, colored

George Baum, fireman

Charles Bow, fireman

King Cade, waiter, colored

George Child, captain of the *Lexington.* Memorial stone in North Burial Ground in Providence, RI.

Jesse Comstock, clerk. Memorial stone in North Burial Ground in Providence, RI

Benjamin Cox, fireman

David Crowley, second mate, Providence * Grave in North Burial Ground, Providence

G. Gilbert, waiter, colored

Oliver Harwell, second cook

Cortland Hempstead, chief engineer ** Buried at Green-Wood Cemetery, Brooklyn, NY

Susan C. Holcomb, chambermaid, colored

Oliver Howell, second cook, colored

John Hoys, baggage master

C. Humber, deckhand

Martin Johnson, wheelman

Benjamin Laden, deckhand **

Joel Lawrence, deckhand

Stephen Manchester, pilot, Providence. * Died in Chicago in 1850; burial site unknown

John Masson, waiter, colored

H.P. Newman, steward **

E. Parkson, waiter, colored

Robert Peters, cook, colored

Isaac Pitman, waiter, colored

William Quimby, second engineer

Henry Reed, coal passer

J. Roslin, waiter, colored

Jos Rustic, waiter, colored

Job Sand, head waiter **

R.B. Shultz, fireman

Charles B. Smith, fireman * Grave in North Burial Ground in Providence, RI.

John H. Tab, waiter, colored

Silas Thorburn or Thurburn, deckhand **

Edward Thurber, first mate ** Grave in North Burial Ground in Providence, RI.

Mr. Walker, bar keeper

Charles Williams, deckhand

George ——, waiter, colored

Solomon ——, waiter, colored

3 deck hands, 1 boy deck hand and 2 wood passers were not identified.

NOTES

Introduction

1. Bleyer, *Long Island and the Sea*, 144–45; New Amsterdam History Center, "Shep Journey: 1656—Prince Maurice—Wrecked on Long Island," https://nahc-mapping.org/mappingNY/encyclopedia/shipjourney/1656-prince-maurice-wrecked-long-island.

1. Early Steamboats on Long Island Sound

2. Bleyer, *Long Island and the Sea*, 127.
3. Ibid., 127–28.
4. "Main Stream of New England."
5. Whittemore, *Past and the Present*, 31–32.
6. Dunbaugh, *Long Island Sound Steamboats*, 2.
7. Brouwer, *Steamboats*, 8–9; Dunbaugh, *Long Island Sound Steamboats*, 2; Weigold, *American Mediterranean*, 37.
8. Dunbaugh, *Night Boat*, 27; Weigold, *American Mediterranean*, 38–39.
9. Brouwer, *Steamboats*, 8–9; Dunbaugh, *Long Island Sound Steamboats*, 2; Weigold, *American Mediterranean*, 37.

2. "Commodore" Cornelius Vanderbilt

10. Lane, *Commodore Vanderbilt*, 8.

11. Ibid., 10–11.
12. Renehan, *Commodore*, 19.
13. Lane, *Commodore Vanderbilt*, 15–17.
14. Ibid, 13–14.
15. Ibid., 15–17.
16. Renehan, *Commodore*, 28.
17. Ibid., 26–27.
18. Lane, *Commodore Vanderbilt*, 18.
19. Ibid., 18, 22–23, 25.
20. Ibid., 26–27.
21. Renehan, *Commodore*, 57–58.
22. Lane, *Commodore Vanderbilt*, 26–27.
23. Ibid., 27, 29.
24. Ibid., 30–32, 34.
25. Renehan, *Commodore*, 70–71.
26. Lane, *Commodore Vanderbilt*, 30–32, 34; Renehan, *Commodore*, 72–73.
27. Lane, *Commodore Vanderbilt*, 40.
28. Ibid., 43–44.
29. Renehan, *Commodore*, 117; Lane, *Commodore Vanderbilt*, 50–52.
30. Ibid.
31. Ibid.
32. Hudson River Maritime Museum, "Historic News: 'General Jackson' Boiler Explosion—Lives Lost and Saved," https://www.hrmm.org/history-blog/historic-news-general-jackson-boiler-explosion-lives-lost-and-saved.
33. Renehan, *Commodore*, 122.
34. "Main Stream of New England."
35. Renehan, *Commodore*, 122–23.
36. Lane, *Commodore Vanderbilt*, 53–54.
37. Ibid., 54–55.
38. Ibid., 55.
39. Ibid., 55–57.
40. Ibid., 57.
41. Ibid., 58–59.
42. Ibid., 60.
43. Ibid., 60–61.
44. Renehan, *Commodore*, 133–34.
45. Ibid.
46. Lane, *Commodore Vanderbilt*, 65.
47. Stiles, *First Tycoon*, 106.
48. Poore, *Perley's Reminiscences*, 39.
49. Renehan, *Commodore*, 134.

3. Construction and Early Operation of the Lexington

50. Stiles, *First Tycoon*, 104–5.

51. Ibid.

52. Brown and Stillwell, *Loss of the Lexington*; *Proceedings of the Coroner*.

53. Brown and Stillwell, *Loss of the Lexington*, 7.

54. Stiles, *First Tycoon*, 104–5.

55. Cussler, *Sea Hunters*, 38–39.

56. Ibid.

57. National Park Service, "West Point Foundry Preserve," https://www. hudsonrivervalley.com/sites/West-Point-Foundry-Preserve-/details. The foundry has an interesting history. It is the only one that survives in some form of the four ironworks selected by President James Madison to supply artillery to the U.S. military. Operating from 1818 to 1911, the foundry, besides building steam engines that powered America's rise as an industrial power, also manufactured some of the nation's first locomotives, ironclad ships, pipes for New York City's water system and, during the Civil War, Parrott guns, cannons with superior range and accuracy. Today, nonprofit Scenic Hudson has transformed the ninety-seven-acre site with ruins of the foundry buildings into an outdoor museum.

58. Cussler, *Sea Hunters*, 38.

59. Stiles, *First Tycoon*, 106.

60. Ibid., 107.

61. Ibid.

62. Ibid., 105.

63. Ibid., 107.

64. Ibid.

65. Renehan, *Commodore*, 136.

66. Stiles, *First Tycoon*, 107–8.

67. Ibid., 108.

68. Renehan, *Commodore*, 136.

69. Lane, *Commodore Vanderbilt*, 65.

70. Stiles, *First Tycoon*, 108.

71. Ibid.

72. Gentile, *Shipwrecks*, 130.

73. Stiles, *First Tycoon*, 109.

74. Lane, *Commodore Vanderbilt*, 66.

75. Stiles, *First Tycoon*, 109.

76. Lane, *Commodore Vanderbilt*, 65.

77. Stiles, *First Tycoon*, 109.

78. Ibid., 110.

79. Ibid., 110, 117.

80. Stiles, *First Tycoon*, 129–30.

81. Dunbaugh, *Long Island Sound Steamboats*, 4.

82. Renehan, *Commodore*, 138–39.

83. Lane, *Commodore Vanderbilt*, 67.

84. Ibid.

85. Ibid., 67–68.

86. Stiles, *First Tycoon*, 122.

87. Ibid., 140.

88. Ibid., 123.

89. Ibid., 123–24.

90. Lane, *Commodore Vanderbilt*, 68.

91. Gentile, *Shipwrecks*, 131

92. Stiles, *First Tycoon*, 129–30.

4. The Last Voyage

93. Hutchinson, "My Grandmother's Story," 159.

94. "Coast Disasters," *Providence Sunday Journal*, November 24, 1895.

95. Connecticut Historical Society Museum & Library, "Captain George Child," http://emuseum.chs.org/emuseum/objects/17240/.

96. Brown and Stillwell, *Loss of the Lexington*, 27.

97. Cussler, *Sea Hunters*, 42.

98. Ibid., 40.

99. Ibid., 41.

100. Find a Grave, "Charles Louis Eberle," https://www.findagrave.com/memorial/174115249/charles-louis-eberle.

101. The Canadian Encyclopedia, "Henry James William Finn," https://www.thecanadianencyclopedia.ca/en/article/henry-james-william-finn; O'Connor, *Death by Fire and Ice*, 61.

102. Cussler, *Sea Hunters*, 41.

103. Casetext, "New Jersey Steam Navigation Company v. Merchants' Bank," https://casetext.com/case/new-jersey-steam-navigation-company-v-merchants-bank/?PHONE_NUMBER_GROUP=P; Fisher, "Birth of the Express Business."

104. Cussler, *Sea Hunters*, 41.

105. Brown and Stillwell, *Loss of the Lexington*, 26–27.

106. Cussler, *Sea Hunters*, 45.

107. Brown and Stillwell, *Loss of the Lexington*, 20.

108. Ibid., 29.

109. Lazell, *Steamboat Disasters*, 194.

110. Cussler, *Sea Hunters*, 47.

111. Lazell, *Steamboat Disasters*, 189.

112. Schenck, "Burning of the Steamboat," 415.

113. Brown and Stillwell, *Loss of the Lexington*, 21.

114. Ibid., 22.

115. Ibid.

116. Ibid., 23.

117. Ibid., 27.

118. Schenck, "Burning of the Steamboat," 416.

119. Brown and Stillwell, *Loss of the Lexington*, 29–30.

120. Schenck, "Burning of the Steamboat," 416.

121. Brown and Stillwell, *Loss of the Lexington*, 18.

122. Ibid.

123. Lazell, *Steamboat Disasters*, 194.

124. Hutchinson, "My Grandmother's Story," 157–58, 161.

125. Ibid.,162.

126. Ibid.

127. Ibid., 164.

128. "A Historical Bale of Cotton," *New York Times*, January 13, 1840.

5. Reaction and Recovery

129. Kierner, *Inventing Disaster*, 179.

130. Cussler, *Sea Hunters*, 52; Hilen, *Letters of Henry Wadsworth Longfellow*, 208–9, 211–13.

131. Stiles, *First Tycoon*, 130.

132. Kierner, *Inventing Disaster*, 179–80.

133. Cussler, *Sea Hunters*, 52.

134. Ibid.

135. Bullock, "Romance and Tragedy."

136. *Long-Island Star*, January 20, 1840, https://bklyn.newspapers.com/image/117448371.

137. "The Sixty Year Echo of a Great Tragedy," *Brooklyn Daily Eagle*, January 14, 1900.

138. Lazell, *Steamboat Disasters*, 214–17.

139. Ibid., 215–17.

140. Shepley, "By Which Melancholy Occurrence," 23–24.

141. Lazell, *Steamboat Disasters*, 223.

142. Ibid., 223–24.

143. Follen Church, "History of Follen Church," https://follen.org/about/history.

144. Lazell, *Steamboat Disasters*, 224–25.

145. Ibid., 226–27.

146. Find a Grave, "George Child," https://www.findagrave.com/memorial/14539338/george-child.

147. Find a Grave, "Edward Thurber," https://www.findagrave.com/memorial/33367972/edward-thurber.

148. Find a Grave, "Jesse Comstock," https://www.findagrave.com/memorial/11705223/jesse-comstock; Laxton, *Hidden History*, 89.

149. O'Connor, *Death by Fire and Ice*, 60.

150. Richman, "Great Gravestone."

151. Find a Grave, "Philo Upson," https://www.findagrave.com/memorial/163508929/philo-upson; Upson Family Association of America, *Upson Family*.

152. Find a Grave, "Jonathan Porter Felt," https://www.findagrave.com/memorial/13607747/jonathan-porter-felt.

153. Find a Grave, "Theophilus Smith," https://www.findagrave.com/memorial/85390697/theophilus-smith.

154. Lost to Sight, "The Swan Brothers," http://losttosight.com/2017/01/the-swan-brothers/.

155. McCarthy, "Steamer Lexington Disaster."

156. Lazell, *Steamboat Disasters*, 168–69.

157. "Disasters to Sound Steamers." *New England Farmer*, April 28, 1866, 3.

158. Find a Grave, "Chester Hillard," www.findagrave.com/memorial/92177797/chester-hillard.

159. "Coast Disasters."

160. Goodyear, "American Paintings," 85.

161. "Mr. Crowley's Retirement," *Providence Daily Journal*, January 19, 1893.

162. Rhode Island Historical Cemeteries, https://rihistoriccemeteries.org/newgravedetails.aspx?ID=214537.

163. "Municipal Court of the City of Providence, October 25, 1900," *Providence Daily Journal*, November 9, 1900.

164. "Steamer Lexington," *Providence Daily Journal*, January 14, 1896.

165. Find a Grave, "Charles Buckingham Smith," https://www.findagrave.com/memorial/125389449/charles-buckingham-smith; Rhode Island Historical Cemeteries, "Charles B. Smith," https://rihistoriccemeteries.org/newgravedetails.aspx?ID=214552.

6. Images of Disaster

166. Kierner, *Inventing Disaster*, 181.

167. Shepley, "By Which Melancholy Occurrence," 1.

168. Kierner, *Inventing Disaster*, 181.

169. Shepley, "By Which Melancholy Occurrence," 2–3.

170. Kierner, *Inventing Disaster*, 181.

171. Shepley, "By Which Melancholy Occurrence," 3.

172. The Met, "About the Met," https://www.metmuseum.org/about-the-met. Lithography is a method of printing originally based on the inability to mix oil and water. An image is etched on a stone or a metal plate with a smooth surface. Ink is applied to a grease-treated image on the flat printing surface while blank areas, which hold moisture, repel the lithographic ink. This inked surface is then printed directly on paper. The process was invented in 1796 by the German author and actor Alois Senefelder and was initially used mostly for musical scores and maps.

173. Shepley, "By Which Melancholy Occurrence," 4.

174. Ibid.

175. Ibid., 4,6.

176. Ibid., 10.

177. Ibid., 14.

178. Bleyer, *Long Island*, 149–52.

179. Shepley, "By Which Melancholy Occurrence," 14, 16.

180. Ibid., 18.

181. Ibid.

182. Ibid.

183. Brust and Shadwell, "Many Versions," 2.

184. Ibid., 4.

185. Ibid.

186. Ibid., 4, 6.

187. Ibid., 6.

188. Ibid.,7.

189. Ibid.

190. Ibid., 8.

191. Ibid., 9.

192. Ibid.

193. Shepley, "By Which Melancholy Occurrence," 19.

194. Brust and Shadwell, "Many Versions," 10; Brust and Shadwell, "Many Versions…An Update," 29.

195. Shepley, "By Which Melancholy Occurrence," 20.

196. Reaves, *American Portrait Prints*, 178.

197. "A Vivid Glimpse of a Lost America," *New York Times*, September 28, 2012.

198. Ibid.

7. The Inquest

199. Brown and Stillwell, *Loss of the Lexington*, 5.

200. Ibid., 5–6.

201. Ibid., 6.

202. Ibid., 7.
203. *Proceedings of the Coroner*, 6–7.
204. Brown and Stillwell, *Loss of the Lexington*, 24.
205. *Proceedings of the Coroner*, 8–14.
206. Brown and Stillwell, *Loss of the Lexington*, 18.
207. Ibid.,12–17.
208. Ibid., 19.
209. Ibid.
210. Ibid., 23.
211. *Proceedings of the Coroner*, 29–31.
212. Ibid., 31–32.
213. Ibid., 34–38.
214. Ibid., 38–39.
215. Ibid., 39.
216. Ibid., 41–42.
217. Ibid., 42–47.
218. Ibid., 47–48.
219. Ibid., 48–52.
220. Ibid., 52–54.
221. Ibid., 54.
222. Ibid.
223. Ibid., 55.
224. Ibid., 55–56.
225. Ibid., 56.
226. Ibid., 57.
227. Ibid., 57–58.
228. Ibid., 70–74.
229. Ibid., 75.
230. Ibid., 76.
231. Ibid., 81.
232. Ibid., 82–87.
233. O'Connor, *Death by Fire and Ice*, 115.

8. The Litigation

234. Justia, "New Jersey Steam Navigation Co. v. Merchants' Banks, 47 U.S. 344 (1848)," https://supreme.justia.com/cases/federal/us/47/344/; "The New Jersey Steam Navigation Company, Respondents and Appellants v. The Merchants' Bank of Boston, Libellants," https://law.resource.org/pub/us/case/reporter/US/47/47.US.344.html.

235. O'Connor, *Death by Fire and Ice*, 125.

9. The Early Salvage Attempts

236. Mutz, *Harrison*, 26–27.

10. The Steamboat Safety Laws

237. U.S. Coast Guard Prevention Blog, https://cgmarinesafety.blogspot. com/2010/07/steamboat-inspection-service.html.
238. Steamboats.org, "Burning of the Ben Sherrod, May 8, 1837," https://www. steamboats.org/archive/9017-2.html.
239. National Archives, Records of the Bureau of Marine Inspection and Navigation, https://www.archives.gov/research/guide-fed-records/groups/041.html.
240. Sandukus, *Gently Down*, 30–31.
241. Ibid., 29.
242. Ibid., 43–46.
243. Ibid., 45.
244. O'Connor, *Death by Fire and Ice*, 148–50; Mystic Seaport Museum, "Steamboat Regulatory Documents," https://research.mysticseaport.org/item/l006405/ l006405-c043; New England Historical Society, "Flashback Photo: Exploding Steamboats Cause Congress to Act," https://www.newenglandhistoricalsociety. com/flashback-photo-exploding-steamboats-cause-congress-act/.

11. Rediscovering the Wreck

245. Cussler, *Sea Hunters*, 56.
246. Ibid.
247. Ibid., 57.
248. Ibid., 58.
249. Barron, "L.I. Divers Find Ship."
250. Cussler, *Sea Hunters*, 59.
251. Email to author from Killian Taylor, Suffolk County Vanderbilt Museum archives and records manager, February 26, 2021.

12. The Lexington Today

252. https://www.facebook.com/Eastern-Search-Survey-109413857123876.
253. Bleyer, "Side-Scan Sonar."

BIBLIOGRAPHY

Barron, James. "L.I. Divers Find Ship Said to Be Vanderbilt's." *New York Times*, October 12, 1983.

Bleyer, Bill. *Long Island and the Sea*. Charleston, SC: The History Press, 2019.

————. "Side-Scan Sonar Illuminates Story of LI's Worst Disaster." *Long Island Boating World*, Parts 1 and 2, August and September 2020.

Brouwer, Norman J. *Steamboats on Long Island Sound*. Charleston, SC: Arcadia Publishing, 2014.

Brown, H.H., and A.H. Stillwell. *Loss of the Lexington, January 13, 1840*. Providence, RI: H.H. Brown and A.H. Stillwell, 1840.

Brust, James, and Wendy Shadwell. "The Many Versions and States of *The Awful Conflagration of the Steam Boat Lexington*." *Imprint: Journal of the American Historical Print Collectors Society* 15, no. 2 (Autumn 1990).

————. "The Many Versions and States of *The Awful Conflagration of the Steam Boat Lexington*. An Update." *Imprint: Journal of the American Historical Print Collectors Society* 18, no. 1 (Spring 1993).

Bullock, C. Seymour. "Romance and Tragedy of Long Island Sound." *Connecticut Magazine*, 1906.

Cussler, Clive. *The Sea Hunters*. New York: Simon & Schuster, 1996.

Dayton, Fred Erving, and John Wolcott Adams. *Steamboat Days*. New York: Frederick A. Stokes Company, 1925.

Dunbaugh, Edwin L. *Long Island Sound Steamboats*. Roslyn, NY: Nassau County Museum of Fine Art, 1984.

————. *Night Boat to New England: 1815–1900*. New York: Greenwood Press, 1992.

Fisher, Charles E. "The Birth of the Express Business." *Bulletin of the Business Historical Society* 13, no. 4 (October 1939): 59–63.

Gentile, Gary. *Shipwrecks of New York*. Philadelphia: Gary Gentile Productions, 1996.

Goodyear, Frank H., Jr. "American Paintings in the Rhode Island Historical Society." *Rhode Island History Journal* 33 (February 1974): 85.

Grohman, Adam. *Claimed by the Sea: Long Island Shipwrecks*. New York: Underwater Historical Research Society, 2008.

Hilen, Andrew, ed. *The Letters of Henry Wadsworth Longfellow*. Vol. 2, *1817–1843*. Cambridge, MA: Belknap Press of Harvard University Press, 1966.

Hutchinson, William Johnston. "My Grandmother's Story." In *Wayside Notes*. New York: W.J. Hutchinson, 1887.

Jenney, Jim. *In Search of Shipwrecks*. New York: A.S. Barnes & Company / Thomas Yoseloff Ltd., 1980.

Keatts, Henry, and George Farr. *The Bell Tolls: Shipwrecks & Lighthouses*. Vol. 2, *Eastern Long Island*. Eastport, NY: Fathom Press, 2002.

Kierner, Cynthia A. *Inventing Disaster*. Chapel Hill: University of North Carolina Press, 2019.

Lane, Wheaton J. *Commodore Vanderbilt: An Epic of the Steam Age*. New York: Alfred A. Knopf, 1942.

Laxton, Glenn V. *Hidden History of Rhode Island: Not-To-Be-Forgotten Tales of the Ocean State*. Charleston, SC: The History Press, 2013.

Lazell, Warren. *Steamboat Disasters and Railroad Accidents in the United States to which Are Appended Accounts of Recent Shipwrecks, Fires at Sea, Thrilling Incidents, etc*. Worcester, MA: Warren Lazell, 1846.

"The Main Stream of New England." *American Heritage* 18, no. 3 (1967).

Maust, Peter E. "Preventing 'Those Terrible Disasters': Steamboat Accidents and Congressional Policy, 1824–1860." Doctoral dissertation, Cornell University, 2012.

McAdam, Roger Williams. *Salts of the Sound*. Brattleboro, VT: Stephen Daye Press, 1939.

McCarthy, Cliff. "Steamer Lexington Disaster." Pioneer Valley History Network's Disasters. https://pvhn3.wordpress.com/1800s/steamer-lexington-disaster/.

Merwin, Daria E. "Maritime History of Southern New England: The View from Long Island." https://www.academia.edu/415974/Maritime_History_of_ Southern_New_England_The_View_from_Long_Island_New_York.

Millard, Candice. *Destiny of the Republic: A Tale of Madness, Medicine, and the Murder of a President*. New York: Doubleday, 2011.

Mitchell, Chelsea. "The Night Disaster Struck in Long Island Sound." Stonington Borough CT, August 1, 2021. https://www.stoningtonboroughct.com/ blog/0821/the-night-disaster-struck-in-long-island-sound.

Mutz, Henry A. *Harrison: The History of a New Jersey Town*. Harrison, NJ: Town of Harrison, 1976.

New England Historical Society. "The SS Lexington Disaster, Worst in Long Island Sound History." https://www.newenglandhistoricalsociety.com/the-ss-lexington-disaster-worst-in-long-island-sound-history/.

O'Connor, Brian E. *Death by Fire and Ice: The Steamboat Lexington Calamity.* Annapolis, MD: Naval Institute Press, 2022.

Poore, Benjamin. *Perly's Reminiscences of Years in the National Metropolis.* Boston: W.A. Houghton & Co., 1886.

Proceedings of the Coroner, in the Case of the Steamer Lexington, Lost by Fire, on the Thirteenth of January, 1840. New York: 1840.

Professional Coin Grading Services. "The Lexington Tragedy." https://www.pcgs.com/news/the-lexington-tragedy.

Reaves, Wendy, ed. *American Portrait Prints.* Charlottesville: University Press of Virginia, 1984.

Renehan, Edward J., Jr. *Commodore: The Life of Cornelius Vanderbilt.* New York: Basic Books, 2007.

Richman, Jeff. "A Great Gravestone, Resurrected." Green-Wood Cemetery, December 7, 2009. https://www.green-wood.com/2009/great-gravestone-resurrected/.

Sandukas, Gregory P. "Gently Down the Stream: How Exploding Steamboat Boilers in the 19th Century Ignited Federal Public Welfare Regulation." Harvard Law School Third Year Paper, 2002.

Schenck, E.H. "Burning of the Steamboat 'Lexington.'" *Magazine of American History*, 1891.

Shepley, Genoa. "By Which Melancholy Occurrence: The Disaster Prints of Nathaniel Currier, 1835–1840." *Panorama: Journal of the Historians of American Art* 1, no. (Fall 2015).

Shipbuilding History. "Jeremiah Simonson, Greenpoint NY." http://shipbuildinghistory.com/shipyards/19thcentury/simonson.htm.

Snow, Edward Rowe. *Great Storms and Famous Shipwrecks of the New England Coast.* Boston: Yankee Publishing Company, 1943.

Springfield Museums. Currier & Ives Collection. https://springfieldmuseums.org.

Stanton, Samuel Ward. *American Steam Vessels.* New York: Smith & Stanton, 1895.

Stiles, T.J. *The First Tycoon: The Epic Life of Cornelius Vanderbilt.* New York: Alfred A. Knopf, 2009.

"Tolling Bell." *Sailors' Magazine*, January 1947.

Upson Family Association of America. *The Upson Family in America.* New Haven, CT: Tuttle, Morehouse & Taylor Company, 1940. https://www.seekingmyroots.com/members/files/G006843.pdf.

U.S. Lighthouse Society, Long Island Chapter. "Execution Rocks Lighthouse." http://www.longislandlighthouses.com/exrock.htm.

Voulgaris, Barbara. "From Steamboat Inspection Service to U.S. Coast Guard: Marine Safety in the United States from 1838–1946." U.S. Department of Defense. https://media.defense.gov/2020/Apr/24/2002288416/-1/-1/0/2009_MARINE_SAFETY_HISTORY_VOULGARIS.PDF.

Weigold, Marilyn E. *The American Mediterranean: An Environmental, Economic and Social History of Long Island Sound*. Port Washington, NY: Kennik Press, 1974.

Whitemore, Henry. *The Past and the Present of Steam Navigation on Long Island Sound*. Providence, RI: Providence and Stonington Steamship Company, 1893.

INDEX

ABOUT THE AUTHOR

 **B**ill Bleyer was a prize-winning staff reporter for *Newsday*, the Long Island daily newspaper, for thirty-three years before retiring in 2014 to write books and freelance for the newspaper and magazines.

He is co-author, with Harrison Hunt, of *Long Island and the Civil War* (The History Press, 2015). He is the author of *Sagamore Hill: Theodore Roosevelt's Summer White House* (The History Press, 2016); *Fire Island Lighthouse: Long Island's Welcoming Beacon* (The History Press, 2017); *Long Island and the Sea: A Maritime History* (The History Press, 2019); and *George Washington's Long Island Spy Ring: A History and Tour Guide* (The History Press, 2021).

His work has been published on Smithsonian.com and in *Civil War News*, *America's Civil War*, *Naval History*, *Sea History*, *Lighthouse Digest* and numerous other magazines and newspapers.

Prior to joining *Newsday*, Bleyer worked at the *Courier-News* in Bridgewater, New Jersey, as an editor and reporter. He began his career as editor of the *Oyster Bay Guardian*.

Bleyer graduated Phi Beta Kappa with highest honors in economics from Hofstra University, where he has been an adjunct professor teaching journalism and economics. He has also been an adjunct professor and lecturer teaching Long Island maritime history at Webb Institute, the naval architecture college in Glen Cove, New York. He earned a master's degree in urban studies at Queens College of the City University of New York.

He lives in Bayville, Long Island.

Visit us at
www.historypress.com
....